Historical Maps of North America

Historical Maps of North America

Michael Swift

PRC

Acknowledgments

The Public Records Office was the source of all the maps used in this book.
Crown Copyright material in the Public Record Office is reproduced by
permission of the Controller of Her Majesty's Stationery Office.
Images are reproduced by courtesy of the Public Record Office.

This edition first published in 2001 by
PRC Publishing Ltd,
Kiln House, 210 New Kings Road,
London SW6 4NZ

© 2001 PRC Publishing Ltd

ISBN 1 85648 592 7

Printed and bound in China

Contents

Introduction

The European Arrival

This is not the place to argue over the semantics of 'discovery'; suffice it to say here that, by the end of the 15th century, circumstances and developments in the old world were such that it became possible for mariners to sail westwards and for contact to be made with the land mass that was to become known as America. There is now little doubt that earlier European travellers, in particular the Vikings from Scandinavia sailing via Iceland and Greenland, had visited north America well before the age of Columbus and Cabot; the major difference between the Viking age and that of the Spaniards, the Portuguese, the English, the French and the other European states involved in the colonisation of the New World is that the Europeans now had the means to secure a domination over the hostile environment — both physical and human — that they encountered.

There were a number of factors which were fundamental in the ability of 16th and 17th century Europeans to sustain their presence in the Americas as opposed to their 10th and 11th century forebears. The first of these was, without doubt, the technological advances in weaponry that had occurred over the previous 500 years. Whilst the Vikings had been armed with weapons — such as swords and spears — which were not wholly dissimilar in destructive power to the weapons that were available to the native population, by the start of the 15th century the Europeans were equipped with guns and armour which made their military effectiveness much greater.

A second factor in the more effective European settlement at the start of the 16th century was that, rather than the small numbers which the Vikings had brought, huge numbers, many of whom were drawn by promises of instant wealth, took the hazardous journey across the Atlantic Ocean. While not all found the gold promised by the promoters of expeditions, once suitable crops — most notably tobacco and sugar — had been identified, so the fertile land became a magnet in itself. The attractiveness of the New World was all the greater during the 16th and 17th century as a result of the religious strife that had affected Europe in the years after the Reformation. Both Protestants and Catholics sought a refuge from persecution in the Old World. Many of the earliest English settlements, for example, were the result of Puritans — a more extreme version of Protestantism than that officially practised in Britain — seeking the space to be able to practise their religion in freedom.

Although there was conflict between the settlers and the natives, for many of the native population the arrival of the Europeans also represented an opportunity for trade. The French in particular saw their role in North America as a conduit through which fur and other commodities could be traded by the native population. As a result, the French-speaking population of North America was ultimately smaller than that speaking English.

Finally, apart from the death and destruction that the Europeans brought with their advanced military equipment, the Europeans also brought death through disease. Many of the most common ailments in Europe, to which the European had developed a toleration, were unknown in the New World and the native population, therefore, had no natural immunity. The arrival of these diseases caused the death of many thousands, weakening yet further the ability of the native tribes to resist the European incursion.

Colonial History

Towards the end of the 15th century, European expansion eastwards had brought India and China, into the European orbit. Trade with these wealthy Oriental countries was becoming increasingly important as a source of prosperity and the European powers were eager to monopolise. At this time, knowledge about the world was still primitive; indeed the accepted wisdom was that the world was flat. It was against this background that Christopher Columbus, an Italian in the service of the Spanish, sailed westwards. His plan was to find an alternative route to the Indies via the west, thereby securing a commercial advantage for his patrons.

It is difficult at this remove to understand just how big was Columbus's step into the unknown. Centuries of stories and speculation meant that his crew's fears were all too present in Columbus's first crossing and, in reality, he came close to being forced to turn round and return to Europe without having achieved success. However, on 12 October 1492 land was sighted — one of the islands, San Salvador, in the chain of islands later known as the Bahamas, and the rest is history. This was the first of four voyages undertaken by Columbus to the area between 1492 and 1504. During these voyages he examined the West Indies — a name derived from his initial belief that he was approaching the Far East — as well as the eastward coast of North and Central America. Although he never physically set foot on the American mainland, the reports that he took back soon circulated and his early explorations were quickly followed by others.

Many European countries had strong seafaring traditions. These included Portugal (whose early maritime exploration of the seas south of Europe, and thence into the Indian Ocean, had been crucial in the opening up of the Far East), England, Spain, Italy and the Netherlands. It is important to remember that, while it is convenient to speak of the nation states as we know them today, the areas that the modern nation states occupy were not so rigid. In Italy, for example, the country was divided up into a huge number of city states, such as Venice, which

were themselves major trading ports. There was also a tradition of the use of mercenaries; thus Columbus, Italian-born, worked for the Spaniards and another Italian, John Cabot (born Giovanni Caboto), was in the service of the English when in 1497/98, he sailed along the coast of Newfoundland and Delaware.

In 1494, under the Treaty of Tordesillas, the Portuguese and the Spanish divided the New World between them. Portugal was granted the territory that was eventually to become Brazil, while Spain was granted the remainder. It was this treaty which unleashed the power of Spain upon Central and South America, power which was to lead to the destruction of the Aztec, Mayan and Incan empires.

The New World was given the name America by the German cartographer Martin Waldeseemüller in 1507 after the Florentine explorer Amerigo Vespucci, who was the first to claim that the New World was a continent. Vespucci was a noted charlatan and his claims were based upon a sensational account of his voyages in which he claimed to have beaten Columbus to the discovery of the New World. Eventually, his claims were disproved but by that time the name 'America' had become accepted. Columbus died in 1506; while he had opened up the New World to European exploration, he died without the wealth that his discoveries were to bring to those who followed.

Initially the Conquistadores from Spain ravaged the Caribbean islands; such was the effect of these invaders that, within the first two decades of the 16th century, the bulk of the native population of the islands was wiped out. Following this, the great wealth on the mainland brought the invaders to Mexico. On 18 November 1518 Hernan Cortes, originally a minor government official on Cuba, landed in what was to become Mexico with a small army of some 600 men. In order to prevent retreat if the going got tough, Cortes ordered that the ships which had transported them be destroyed. At this time, the native Aztec empire was ruled by Montezuma and the scene was set for a struggle between two inspiring leaders.

The Spanish, however, held several major advantages. First, in technological terms, they possessed guns and gunpowder, which were unknown to the Aztecs. Likewise, the use of armoured horses was alien to the native population. Finally, to the Aztecs, the Spaniards appeared like their god Quetzacoatl and, as a result, were treated as demigods. It was only gradually that the Aztecs learned their mistake and by that time the Spanish forces were already well in command.

The conquest of Mexico was the staging post for a further attack upon the South American natives, when the Incan empire, ruled by Atahualpa, was defeated by a new Spanish army led by Francisco Pizarro. To the north of Mexico City, Francisco Vasquez de Coronado headed along the coast, founding the city of Huepac in 1540 and capturing the city of Moho Pueblo after an 80-day siege in 1541. At the same time Hernando de Alarcon explored the Colorado River and Garcia Lopez de Cardenas discovered the Grand Canyon.

The growing Spanish presence was reflected in the founding of towns and cities that are still important today. On Cuba, both Havana and Santiago were established in 1514. Panama, from where Pizarro set sail in 1531, was established in 1519, while in South America Quito was founded in 1534, Lima in 1535 and Bogota in 1539.

South and Central America were not the only destinations explored and conquered by the Spanish. In 1513 Juan Ponce de Leon discovered Florida; it was in Florida that the first long-lasting Spanish colonial settlement in North America — known today as St Augustine — was founded by Pedro Menendez in 1565. From Florida between 1539 and 1543 Hernando do Soto explored the coast of the Gulf of Mexico as far as the Mississippi before heading inland to the future states of Arkansas and Oklahoma.

Spanish and Portuguese activity was largely concentrated at this time in Central and South America; further north it was the French who took the leading role in the opening up of the New World. It is in 1524 that Giovanni da Verrazano, a Florentine employed by the French, explored the east coast of North America. In all likelihood, he was the first European to sail into the future Hudson River. Ten years later, in 1534, Jacques Cartier discovered the St Lawrence River. Cartier sailed up the St Lawrence as far as the site of the future city of Montreal, hoping to discover the elusive northwest passage that would provide access to the riches of the Far East. In the event he found no wealth on the scale of that found by the Spaniards and Portuguese and returned home finally in 1542.

Unlike the Spanish and Portuguese the other European nations did not find great treasures in the New World and so were happy to trade with the native population of North America: there was not the same impetus to conquest. The English, in particular, were happy to concentrate during the 16th century on authorised piracy, robbing the Spanish treasure ships as they sailed from Central America through the Caribbean. One factor in the Spanish development of Florida was as a strategic defensive measure against these English pirates.

French involvement with North America started shortly after the discovery of Newfoundland. Temporary settlements were established to cure and dry the fish (primarily cod) caught close to the mainland. This trade was developed further by trade with the native Americans in fur; again, however, this did not require the creation of permanent bases. In the 1530s, Jacques Cartier endeavoured to establish a permanent colony at Quebec, but this was to fail, with the result that the first French colony was established by the noted explorer Samuel de Champlain (1570-1635), whose name was to be perpetuated in name of Lake Champlain, at Quebec in 1608. The foundation of Quebec was followed in 1642 by that of Montreal. In this area the French developed a strong trade based on the export of fur. It was also from Quebec that French explorers took European intervention into the North American heartland. In 1673, Jacques Marquette, a Jesuit, and Louis Joliet headed southwards to the Mississippi, claiming the whole river for the French. Nine years later, in 1682, Rene Robert Cavelier, Sieur de la Salle, continued the southward exploration of the Mississippi River, finally reaching its delta. He claimed the area for France, christening the region Louisiana after the French king, Louis XIV, the 'Sun King'. In 1718, another Frenchman, Jean-Baptiste Le Moyne, Sieur de Bienville (1680-1768), founded the city of Nouvelle Orleans (better known today as New Orleans).

While the French were establishing themselves on the St Lawrence and down the Mississippi, other developments were occurring on the eastern seaboard. In 1609, Henry Hudson, an Englishman employed by the Dutch East India Company, to look for the elusive north west passage, sailed up a river — the future Hudson River — and claimed the territory for the Dutch. Nieuw (New) Holland was established around Long Island Sound in 1614 and, 12 years later in 1626, one of the great land deals in history saw Peter Minuit purchase the island of Manhattan from the local Indians. The area, which was named Nieuw Amsterdam, is believed to have cost no more than the equivalent of 24 dollars. Also established by the Dutch was Fort Orange further upstream the Hudson River; this was later to be renamed Albany by the British and is still the capital of New York State. The Dutch presence in the New World was, however, destined to be shortlived, as the European rivalry between the Netherlands and Britain resulted in the latter seizing the Dutch-occupied region in August 1664 and rechristening it New York. The Dutch governor at the time was Peter Stuyvesant. The primary Dutch reason for settlement was trade and, thus, the actual number of Dutch settlers was few; unlike other nations, Dutch arrivals were normally employees of the sponsoring company — in this case the Dutch West Indies Company — and received no grants of land. Apart from the Dutch, representatives of a number of other European nations, including Swedes and Germans, also lived in New Holland, as did some English Puritans who had settled on Long Island. After the Dutch surrendered in 1664, their nationals were allowed to remain in the country.

Of all the major players in the colonisation of the Americas, it was the English (and later the British) that were the last to make their presence felt but were, ultimately, to become the dominant European power in North America and in the West Indies. Although English support had seen Cabot discover Newfoundland relatively early on, domestic troubles meant that England's primary concern at this time was its own security. The Reformation, consequent rejection of Catholicism, and weak monarchs after Henry VIII — Edward VI was but a child when he inherited the throne and died a teenager; Mary's Catholicism and marriage to King Philip II of Spain brought controversy and internal strife — led to the almost constant threat of European intervention. This culminated, following the succession of Protestant Elizabeth I, in the Spanish Armada.

This is not to say that England ignored the New World; rather than acting to acquire land English sailors, most notably figures like Sir Walter Raleigh, acted as pirates, seizing the treasure that the Spaniards had looted from South and Central America. In 1583 Sir Humphrey Gilbert took possession of Newfoundland in the name of Queen Elizabeth I, but this ownership was shortlived and no effort was made to establish a permanent settlement. The first English attempt to establish a permanent colony was in North Carolina — the ill-fated Roanoke Island settlement founded by Sir Walter Raleigh in 1585. Raleigh christened the region Virginia after Queen Elizabeth I — the Virgin Queen.

The first settlers, led by Sir Richard Grenville, landed in the autumn of that year, but were soon deserted by their leader who returned to England. During his brief stay in North America, Grenville had alienated the local Indians by destroying a native village. During the winter of 1585/86, the settlers were left to fend for themselves; no supplies were received and, when Raleigh arrived during the spring of 1586, the surviving colonists returned to England. Raleigh attempted a further settlement in 1587, which initially seemed more successful. However, the colonists' leader, John White, was forced to return to England later the same year to seek further provisions. At the time White returned to England, all the available ships were required in the war against Spain — culminating in the defeat of the Armada in 1588 — and none were available to replenish the colony. Ships finally returned to Roanoke in 1590 but, by that date, although there was evidence of the colony there was no trace of the colonists themselves.

The next phase in the English colonisation of North America came with the establishment of Jamestown in 1607, when 105 settlers arrived under the command of Captain John Smith. This settlement was to form the basis of the province of Virginia. The origin of this settlement was the granting of a Royal Charter by King James I on 10 April 1606 to the London Company. Led by Sir Thomas Smythe, this company soon changed its name to the Virginia Company in order to exploit the expected riches in the area. In December 1606 three ships — the *Susan Constant*, the *Discovery* and the *Godspeed* — sailed for the New World. The initial promise, however, soon turned into a near disaster. Although Jamestown was built some 30 miles up the James River on a peninsula, as a defensive measure against local Indians, none of the expected wealth materialised. In place came internal dissent and, without the inspired leadership of John Smith, it is almost certain that the colony would have failed. Even so, further problems — including the enforced return of Smith to England after catching a virulent illness and the loss of supply ships — meant that Jamestown continued to teeter. One factor alone — the commercial exploitation of tobacco — was to lead to the eventual success of the enterprise. Even this traffic was, however, initially threatened; James I was an ardent opponent of smoking — indeed wrote a tract against it — but the traffic (and the tax revenues it generated) was allowed to continue. Further trade was encouraged by Sir Edwin Sandys, who promoted by various means, the cultivation of sugar and cotton as well as the exploitation of the natural resources of the land. It was in 1619 that the first black Africans arrived in the new English colony; at this time they had travelled across the Atlantic of their own free will — it was not until 1650 that slave-owning was officially permitted.

Following the successful — ultimately — settlement of Virginia, other English colonies were soon authorised or established. Of these earlier settlements, it was the arrival of the Pilgrim Fathers, the 102 Puritans on board the *Mayflower*, who landed in November 1620 at Cape Cod, in the future Massachusetts that was the most significant. These settlers, emigrating from England in order to be able to practise better their Protestant faith, signed the Mayflower Compact. This agreement promised that the settlers would be obedient to the laws of the leaders. This established the principle of government by the people, one of the basis principles of democracy. In November 1621, the Pilgrim Fathers celebrated their first harvest in the New World, a celebration which continues each November to this day through Thanksgiving Day. Boston was itself founded in 1630.

Further colonies followed. In 1623 New Hampshire was founded, although its early history was inexorably interlinked with neighbouring Massachusetts. In 1629 King Charles I granted to Robert Heath the colony of Carolina; this had originally been Spanish and was later to be divided into North and South Carolina. The town of Portsmouth, destined to be the colony's (and state's) capital until 1808, was founded in 1630. This was followed in 1634 by the creation of Maryland.

Just as the founding of Massachusetts was the result of religious strife in England, so too that of Maryland; the difference here was that Maryland was a refuge for the persecuted Catholic population. Although England was nominally a Protestant country, King Charles I was suspected of having leanings towards the Catholic faith — indeed his French wife, Henrietta Maria, was a Catholic (she was the sister of the French King Louis XIII) — and the perceived drift towards Catholicism at the court (reflected in the number of high profile conversions) was one factor in the deterioration of relations between the King and Parliament, which culminated in the English Civil War (1642-49). The leading light in the creation of the new colony was Leonard Calvert in 1632 and the first 200 Catholic refugees arrived two years later; complete religious freedom was guaranteed in 1649. The Calvert family was to have a dominant role in the colony's affairs right through to Independence.

Further English colonies followed. Connecticut was established in 1635 and Rhode Island in 1636. The same year witnessed the foundation of Harvard College in Massachusetts, a further example that English settlement was well and truly taking root. English power was further enhanced by the take-over in 1664 of Nieuw Amsterdam, Nieuw Holland and Delaware from the Dutch. The last-named state, originally investigated by John Cabot in 1498, was first settled permanently by Swedes in 1635 as Ny Sverige (New Sweden); Swedish rule was, however, shortlived, and in 1655 control passed to the Dutch. Delaware was, from 1682 until 1775, incorporated into Pennsylvania. Pennsylvania itself was founded by the Quaker William Penn in 1681, whilst Philadelphia, Pennsylvania's state capital, followed two years later. The last of the English 'Thirteen Colonies' — Georgia — was established by James Oglethorpe in 1732.

Completely separate to the creation of these 'Thirteen Colonies' along the New England coast was the English development of north Canada through the Hudson Bay Company. This company was launched in 1669 and established trading posts from where fur and other goods were exported to Britain. The first Governor of the Hudson Bay Company, in 1670, was Prince Rupert, who had been one of the main leaders of the Royalist army during the English Civil War.

With the rise of British power on the New England coast and in the north of Canada posing a threat to the French dominance along the St Lawrence and the Mississippi, it was inevitable that there would be rivalry between European neighbours.

On the western seaboard, following the earlier exploration of the coast of California, it was only in the mid- and late 18th century that explorers sailed further north. The crucial figure in the exploration of the sea between California and the Arctic Circle was a Dane employed by the Russians, after whom the straits between Alaska and Russia were named. It was through Vitus Bering that the Russians came to have a presence in North America.

The coast of the area known later as Oregon Country was sailed in 1778 by Captain James Cook, one of the most famous of all the late

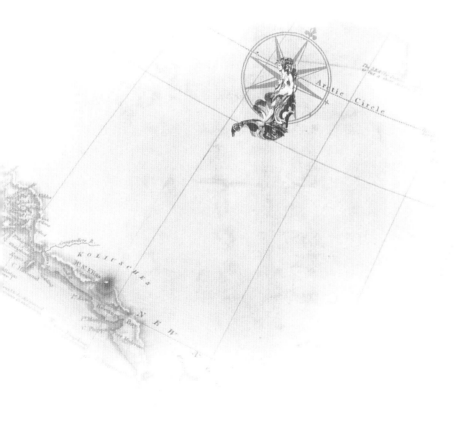

18th century British explorers, a crucial figure in the development of British influence in the Pacific. George Vancouver followed Cook in 1792. Land exploration was pursued after 1804 by Meriweather Lewis and William Clark, from which British control of this region developed.

Anglo-French Conflict

Throughout the Middle Ages, England and France had been at war; partly this was a reflection of the fact that the inter-relationship of the royal families and the powerful barons of both realms meant that the English monarch could claim the throne of France and vice versa. It was only in the mid-16th century that England finally lost its last permanent foothold on the European mainland, when Calais — forever engrained on the heart of Queen Mary — was surrendered to the French (although this did not mark the end of English involvement in warfare along the Channel coast). It was inevitable as both England (and later the United Kingdom) and France developed overseas empires that friction would ensue between the two. Often this friction was an adjunct to the major wars that afflicted Europe from 1660 onwards, but even when peace existed nominally in Europe, in the colonies strife could continue unabated. In North America, this rivalry had two immediate consequences. First, both Britain and France constructed a network of forts to defend their territory and, second, alliances were forged with potentially friendly native tribes in order to gain a tactical advantage.

The first major European war between Britain and France to have consequences in the New World was during the first decade of the 18th century. In Europe, there was concern about the growing power of the French state under Louis XIV and, in 1702, Britain under Queen Anne, joined the Grand Alliance against France and the latter's ally, Spain. Known as the War of Spanish Succession, the war in Europe was to culminate in the French defeat at the Battle of Blenheim. In North America British forces, allied with Indian tribes, attacked the Spanish missions in Florida during 1702 and 1703, destroying 13 of the 14 then established. The town of St Augustine was also besieged and destroyed. In the north, French attacks launched from Montreal and Quebec led to assaults on the British-held settlements in New York State, such as Albany, and the northeastern seaboard. The French also captured two of the British settlements established on the north coast of

Newfoundland, Bonavista (in 1704) and St John's (1708). In 1710 the British countered the French assaults by launching a naval attack against Nova Scotia, capturing Port Royal, and down the St Lawrence, where a British naval assault against Quebec foundered in fog. The War of Spanish Succession ended in 1713 with the Treaty of Utrecht; this treaty saw France cede a great deal of territory in Canada to the British. In particular the huge hinterland round Hudson Bay, Newfoundland and Acadia (the area to the north of the 'Thirteen Colonies') passed to British rule, immeasurably strengthening the British position in the region.

For the French, the Treaty of Utrecht was a watershed. Their colonial possessions in North America, strung along the St Lawrence and the Mississippi, were now sandwiched between two areas dominated by the English — the Hudson Bay region and New England — and the British colonies were both more populous and better organised in terms of manufacturing industry.

The next European war to have an impact on North America was the War of Austrian Succession between 1743 and 1748, which is known as King George's War in North America. In June 1745 the colonial army under William Pepperrell achieved a major victory when it captured the French fort at Louisbourg. This major fortification, situated on Cape Breton Island (to the north of Acadia [Nova Scotia] which had been ceded to Britain in 1713) was of major strategic importance in defending the sealanes into the Gulf of St Lawrence. Much to colonial displeasure, the British government allowed the French to reclaim Cape Breton Island after the Treaty of Aix-la-Chapelle, which settled the war.

After this war, the French decided to strengthen their position to the west of New England and in the early 1750s seized control of the Ohio Valley, building forts; such as that at Fort Duquesne, Pittsburgh at the same time. In Europe an uneasy peace existed between Britain and France, in North America the British decided to take unilateral action against the French. Virginian troops under the control of George Washington established their own presence at Fort Necessity close to Fort Duquesne. However, this intervention was poorly supported and the colonial base was destroyed on 3 July 1754. This was not to be the end of the colonial efforts to dislodge the French and, in the following year, a further expedition under the control of General Edward Braddock suffered a major defeat at French hands.

By this date, European tension was again to the fore and in 1756 the Seven Years' War broke out. Known as the French and Indian Wars in North America, this conflict was to witness the almost total elimination of French power in North America. Louisbourg was again captured (on 26 July 1758) and French forces were forced out of forts at Duquesne, Ticonderoga, Crown Point and Niagara as they retreated towards Quebec. The most crushing blow came on 13 September 1759 when British forces under General James Wolfe finally captured Quebec.

The Treaty of Paris, signed on 10 February 1763, effectively ended French influence on the American mainland and was a reflection of the military weakness so cruelly exposed on the battlefield. France ceded all of Canada to the British, along with all land to the east of the Mississippi. Britain also gained Florida from Spain. France, however, retained its colonial possessions in the Caribbean and two small islands — St Pierre and Miquelon — just to the south of Newfoundland.

The Prelude to Independence

With the defeat of the French and the increased possessions granted by the Treaty of Paris, British power in North America was now at its peak. However, the cost of the war was such that the means of paying for it and reducing the national debt became critical. In addition to the financial constraints, there was an increasing unwillingness on the part of the colonists to be seen as anything other than the equals of the British establishment.

The next decade was to witness a gradual deterioration in relations between the colonists and the British authorities, a deterioration which was to culminate in the Declaration of Independence of 1776 and the subsequent war. From 1764 until 1767 a number of measures to raise taxation were imposed from London. The colonists already felt that their commercial position was undermined by the Navigation Acts of 1660, which gave British ships a monopoly of trade to and from the mother country; this feeling was compounded by the fact that there were no representatives of the colonies in London to fight their corner strongly in the corridors of power.

Thus, when a series of taxation measures emerged in the mid-1760s — the Currency Act (prohibiting the colonies from issuing their own money), the Sugar Act (imposing a new duty on sugar), the Stamp Act (which required all legal documents and printed papers to be 'stamped'; this was repealed in 1766), the Quartering Act (which required the colonies to pay for the costs of the British military garrison) and the Townshend Acts (which imposed duties on a whole range of goods) — colonial dissatisfaction grew dramatically. Many of the measures were rejected through a form of passive resistance while, in November 1767, representatives from nine colonies met in New York to demand 'No taxation without representation '.

Apart from the issue of taxation, the colonists were further aggrieved by the fact that, after the Treaty of Paris in 1763 had granted Britain much of the land to the west of the 'Thirteen Colonies' to the Mississippi, the British had issued a proclamation defining the westward limits of the existing colonies — the so-called Proclamation Line — which reserved all the land to the west of this to the crown. The colonists felt that this restriction arbitrarily removed the opportunities that the existing colonies had for expansion. This again was interpreted as an arbitrary decision upon which the colonists had had no influence.

The situation continued to deteriorate. On 5 March 1770 three civilians were killed by British troops in Boston. The causes of this 'Boston Massacre' are uncertain, but it is probable that a local crowd got out of hand and the nervous troops reacted with gunfire. Whatever the causes, the event showed the great volatility in the 'Thirteen Colonies' at this time. On 16 December 1775, the Boston Tea Party saw rioting citizens dispose of vast quantities of tea into the harbour as a further rejection of British taxation. The British government responded with a number of punitive measures, including the closure of Boston harbour. The result of this was the first Continental Congress, when representatives of twelve of the 'Thirteen Colonies', the exception was Georgia, met in Philadelphia. This congress resolved to cease trade with Britain and its other colonies. In early 1775 the situation deteriorated further with the first actual combat between British soldiers — the Redcoats — and the American militia — the Minutemen — at Concord and Lexington. The latter were so called because they were ready to react immediately to a call to action.

A second Continental Congress met and, on 15 June 1775, George Washington was appointed commander-in-chief. However, militarily things did not start well for the revolutionaries as their forces were defeated at the Battle of Bunker Hill two days later. The scene was now set for the formal Declaration of Independence, which came from the Congress at Philadelphia on 4 July 1776.

The Revolutionary War

The military campaign that marked the American War of Independence saw both sides gain and lose the advantage. Initially Washington had had success in driving the British out of Boston on 4 March 1776 and British troops were never to return to Massachusetts thereafter. However, Washington was defeated on Long Island in the following August. This reverse was, however, to be revenged when he defeated British forces at Trenton and Princeton after having crossed the frozen Delaware River. These victories were significant because they secured the rebel positions in Pennsylvania and New Jersey, both of which had threatened by British forces. British successes at this time included the capture of New York.

In 1777 British forces under General Sir William Howe captured Philadelphia, but the grandiose plan envisaged by General John Burgoyne of sending 7,000 British and allied soldiers southwards from Canada to bisect the rebel forces came to nothing. Burgoyne's advance was too slow to take the rebels by surprise and, with his supply lines cut and with his rations all but exhausted, he was forced to surrender the remnant of his army at Saratoga on 17 October.

This American victory was to have profound implications; both France and Spain, were eager to capitalise on a wounded Britain, declared war and this had the effect of forcing Britain to contemplate war not only in North America but in Europe and in its other colonies. In previous wars against France, Britain had always been part of a European alliance which had ensured that the European theatre was in the hands of other nations, leaving Britain to fight France at sea and in the colonies. In this war, Britain stood alone and could ill afford to fight France and Spain single-handed.

The threat of a near global war forced Britain to offer terms to the rebels; they could have virtually everything they wanted, except independence. Needless to say, with the rebels now appearing to have the upper hand, this offer was rejected and the war continued. British forces were forced to evacuate Philadelphia but this was countered by a successful British invasion at Charleston on 12 May 1780. The following year, the British army under General Charles Cornwallis withdrew to Yorktown in Virginia. A French fleet commanded by Admiral de Grasse landed French troops in North America; these forces, led by General Rochambeau, combined with American forces under Washington to defeat Cornwallis's army at Yorktown on 19 October 1781. This defeat effectively marked the end of the War of Independence.

A preliminary peace treaty was agreed at Versailles in France on 30 November 1782 and a formal Treaty of Versailles was signed on 3 September 1783. This treaty guaranteed the independence of the 'Thirteen Colonies' and also transferred the lands acquired by Britain from France after 1763 south of the Great Lakes. Britain returned Florida to Spain. However, Britain retained Nova Scotia and the rest of Canada. In addition, some 100,000 loyalists also migrated northwards, forsaking their original homes in North America to retain links with the British crown.

Although the Treaty of Versailles had established the independence of the 'Thirteen Colonies', the final state of the newly independent land had still to be finalised. In addition, there were a number of territorial disputes outstanding with Britain; these were to rumble on until the middle of the following century and led to one further war between the two countries and to potential conflict on at least one other occasion.

The Spanish in California

California was first explored by the Portuguese in 1542 when Cabrilho sailed along the Pacific coast and in 1700 it was established by a Jesuit priest that the area was not an island. However, it was not until 1769 that the Spaniards gradually expanded northward from Mexico primarily to prevent an expected British take-over. The first settlement to be created was San Diego, in 1769. A total of 21 missions were established along the Californian coast; including Santa Barbara in 1786, San Miguel in 1797 and San Francisco in 1776. These missions were designed to bring Christianity to the large native Indian population from the number of tribes (including the Hoka, the Aztek-Tano and the Penuti), and some 15,000 Indians were housed in these missions. Los Angeles was founded in 1778.

In 1821 California was incorporated into Mexico, which had become independent from Spain during the same year. In 1846, when war broke out between the United States and Mexico, California sought to achieve independence. However, following the Treaty of Guadalupe Hidalgo of 1848, California was incorporated into the USA. Almost immediately, the arrival of new settlers — many of whom were inspired by the first gold rushes — forced the Indians out of the surviving missions. California became the 31st state of the Union on 9 September 1850.

The Growth of the Union

Following the Treaty of Paris, which settled the War of Independence, the form of the new nation was still not finalised. Of the original 'Thirteen Colonies' of New England there was no definite agreement as to the nature of the post-colonial era. Within each state there were those who argued for a federal structure and those who argued for the independence of each individual colony. On 25 May 1787 the Constitutional Convention opened in Philadelphia. For the next four months, the convention argued about the new constitution before agreeing, on 17 September, to promote a federal structure. Each former colony had to then ratify the new constitution. The first state to ratify the constitution was Delaware on 7 December 1787 and the last was Rhode Island on 29 May 1790. Apart from the original colonies, the United States also included the territories to the east of the Mississippi, such as Kentucky and Tennessee, which had been previously French, but were ceded to Britain in 1763. These were only gradually to achieve statehood: Kentucky in 1792, Tennessee in 1796, Ohio in 1803, Mississippi in 1817 and Alabama in 1819.

Even after the War of Independence, there were areas, in particular those that were later to form the states of Michigan, Illinois and Indiana, where the British claimed jurisdiction. These lands were only ceded to the USA in 1795 after the Jay Treaty. Known initially as the Northwest Territory, these regions were gradually carved into new states and the native Indian population subjugated.

The next stage in the territorial expansion of the USA was the Louisiana Purchase of 1803. Although originally this region had been controlled by France, it had been ceded to Spain during the Seven Years' War. In 1800 France regained sovereignty; however, in 1803 the Emperor Napoleon sold the region for $15 million.

Further expansion saw the Mississippi delta annexed from Spain in 1810 and 1812. This acquisition was followed in 1819 when Spain ceded three further territories to the United States. These were Florida, the acquisition of which was ratified in 1821, the area of Louisiana to the west of the Mississippi delta and the southwestern part of the future state of Oklahoma.

In the north, improved relations with the British saw the regularisation of the US-Canadian border along the 49th parallel in 1818; this saw Britain cede the northern part of North Dakota and Minnesota to the United States and gain an area to the north of Montana in compensation. The next major development was the Webster-Ashburton Treaty with Britain in 1842; this regularised the border of Maine and Canada, seeing the state expand to the north up to Fort Kent, and also the section of Minnesota along the coast of Lake Superior. The last US-British territorial settlement concerned Oregon Country — the region which was to form the future states of Washington, Oregon, Idaho and the western part of Montana — which had been jointly held by Britain and the United States since 1818 and which was transferred to US sovereignty in 1846. Although the settlement was achieved peacefully, the dispute over this region — with the British fearing that the USA would seek jurisdiction as far north as the 54th parallel — was the closest that Britain and the United States came to war after 1812.

Further south, the largely English-speaking settlers of Texas had revolted against their Mexican overlords in 1835. A Texan Republic was declared on 2 March 1836. The constitution of the new republic was largely based upon that adopted by the United States at the end of the 18th century. Following this declaration of independence, war broke out between the settlers and the Mexican authorities, who were eager to see their powers restored. It was during this war that the famous battle at the Alamo took place, when a small rebel force held out against a numerically much larger Mexican army. Although this battle has passed into United States mythology, it did not proceed quite as the film would have us believe! Not all the rebels were killed in the battle; a number, including Davy Crockett, survived and were later executed, while the rebel forces had the advantage of holding a strong fortress against a largely conscript and untrained government army. The defeat at the Alamo was followed by a massacre at Goliad of some 350 rebels. This spurred the Texan army under General Sam Houston to attack the Mexican army, which was defeated on 21 April 1836, after which Texan independence was recognised. The United States recognised Texan independence in July 1836 but, on 25 August 1837, turned down an initial approach for the new republic to be annexed to join the union. The 'Lone Star Republic' was, however, only to have a short independent life; on 29 December 1845 it was admitted to the union as the 28th state. Part of its territory was to form the eastern section of New Mexico while part became southwestern Kansas.

The annexation of Texas caused war to break out between Mexico and the United States. Following the annexation, it was claimed that the US-Mexican border would be now formed by the Rio Grande and not the Nueces River, which had been regarded as the border up until that point. The US authorities also objected to a Mexican prohibition on the further migration of English-speaking settlers into California. On 8 March 1846, United States forces led by General Zachary Taylor crossed the Nueces into the disputed territory between that river and the Rio Grande. Following the death of 11 Americans on 25 April 1846, the United States declared war on Mexico on 11 May. American land forces quickly invaded in the north of California, where settlers revolted at Sonoma (the Bear Flag Revolt of 14 June 1846), just to the north of San Francisco. Other insurrections took place along the Gila River, where victory was achieved at San Gabriel (8 January 1847) despite defeat at San Pasqual (6 December 1846), and in the south where victories were achieved at, inter alia, Monterrey (21-24 September 1846), Buena Vista (22/23 February 1847) and Chapultepec (13 September 1847) saw the United States achieve ultimate victory. By the end of the war, their forces had occupied many of the major Mexican cities, including Mexico City itself, San Francisco, Santa Barbara, Santa Fe, Albuquerque and Veracruz. The war was settled by the Treaty of Guadalupe Hidalgo, which became effective on 4 July 1848; for the price of $15 million, the USA acquired California and New Mexico, while the Mexican authorities also waived all claims on Texas. The final border settlement in this region came with the Gadsen Purchase of 1852, when the USA acquired the southernmost parts of New Mexico and Arizona.

The last of the United States's major land acquisitions on the mainland of North America came with the purchase of Alaska from the Russians in 1867.

The Growth of the States — A Case Study

Although the date of foundation of most states is well established, the confirmation of each individual state's boundaries was not necessarily predetermined at foundation. This was particularly true in the case of the earliest colonies established in North America by the British, where the western boundaries of many of the original Thirteen Colonies was not finalised until after the Declaration of Independence. Moreover, it is important to remember that, until the establishment of the United States and the acceptance of the United States' constitution by each of the subscribing states, there were many examples of disputes between neighbouring colonies.

This section looks at the development of the state of Pennsylvania, since the growth of this state is typical of the way that many of the early colonies became established.

Prior to the first grant of land to William Penn, part of the land that was to form the modern-day state of Pennsylvania was claimed — by Connecticut in the north, and in the south by Maryland and Virginia. Penn's first grant covered land in the extreme southeast of the future state, comprising the original counties of Bucks, Chester and Philadelphia. Between the date of the colony's foundation and 1700, there were some 15 purchases of land from the local Native American tribes that gradually extended the area of European influence — but not necessarily European occupation — through much of the future state. For example, on 14 July 1683 there were two purchases of land covering territory between the Schuylkill and Chester rivers, and between the Schuylkill and Pemmapecka rivers. A further four land purchases occurred between 1701 and 1726 before the creation of the fourth county — Lancaster — in 1729. This new county was carved partly out of the earlier Chester County but also out of land beyond the original area of occupation.

A further 20 years was to elapse before the creation of the next county — York — in 1749. This new county was carved out of Lancaster County. Between 1750 and 1773 a further six counties were created, again all with very British names such as Cumberland. This gradually extended European influence north and west from the original settlements. Alongside these counties, between 1732 and 1768 there were a further nine land purchases. One of these, signed at Fort Stanwix on 5 November 1768 and called the 'New Purchase', covered land from the northeast to the southwest of the state.

It is interesting to note that the British influence on the choice of names for the new counties created after Independence disappeared, with the new creations commemorating both the heroes of the Revolution and the French sympathisers of it. Thus, the 12th County to be created, in 1782, was called Washington, while others were called Fayette and Franklin. In 1784 came two more deeds confirming additional land and the borders of the state. Of these, that on 23 October was the deed which saw the purchase of the northwest of the state — this was known as the 'Last Purchase'. The final land purchase came on 3 March 1793 when the triangle of land at the extreme northwest of the state, bounding onto Lake Erie, was purchased. As with most of these purchases, the land was bought from the local Native American tribes.

Alongside the purchase of land came the creation of further counties. By 1850, the total number of counties within Pennsylvania had reached 63, and this was to rise to 67 by 1878. Initially, the creation of new counties occurred as previously unsettled land was occupied, but by the early years of the 19th century the process of settlement was such that new counties had to be carved out of older counties.

This is an inevitably attenuated account of the development of one individual colony and state, but the broad history of its growth is mirrored by the development of others throughout the USA.

The States of the Union

1	**Delaware** 9 December 1787	32	**Minnesota** 11 May 1858	
2	**Pennsylvania** 12 December 1787	33	**Oregon** 14 February 1859	
3	**New Jersey** 18 December 1787	34	**Kansas** 29 January 1861	
4	**Georgia** 2 January 1788	35	**West Virginia** 20 June 1863	
5	**Connecticut** 9 January 1788	36	**Nevada** 31 October 1864	
6	**Massachusetts** 6 February 1788	37	**Nebraska** 1 March 1867	
7	**Maryland** 28 April 1788	38	**Colorado** 1876	
8	**South Carolina** 23 May 1788	39	**North Dakota** 2 November 1889	
9	**New Hampshire** 21 June 1788	40	**South Dakota** 2 November 1889	
10	**Virginia** 25 June 1788	41	**Montana** 8 November 1889	
11	**New York** 26 July 1788	42	**Washington** 11 November 1889	
12	**North Carolina** 21 November 1789	43	**Idaho** 3 July 1890	
13	**Rhode Island** 29 May 1790	44	**Wyoming** 10 July 1890	
14	**Vermont** 4 March 1791	45	**Utah** 4 January 1896	
15	**Kentucky** 1 June 1792	46	**Oklahoma** 16 November 1907	
16	**Tennessee** 1 June 1796	47	**New Mexico** 6 January 1912	
17	**Ohio** 1 March 1803	48	**Arizona** 1912	
18	**Louisiana** 30 April 1812	49	**Alaska** 1959	
19	**Indiana** 11 December 1816	50	**Hawaii** 1959	
20	**Mississippi** 10 December 1817			
21	**Illinois** 3 December 1818			
22	**Alabama** 1819			
23	**Maine** 15 March 1820			
24	**Missouri** 10 August 1821			
25	**Arkansas** 15 June 1836			
26	**Michigan** 26 January 1837			
27	**Florida** 1845			
28	**Texas** 29 December 1845			
29	**Iowa** 28 December 1846			
30	**Wisconsin** 29 May 1849			
31	**California** 9 September 1850			

The Cartography

The Reasons for the Cartography

There were a number of factors that led to the vast output of maps on America and the West Indies from the early 16th century onward. First, the discovery of the Americas was contemporaneous with that glorious period of European learning known as the Renaissance. Science, art and literature all flourished; many of the existing precepts of knowledge were being questioned. No longer, for example, was the world at the centre of the universe as astronomy showed conclusively the rotation of the planets around the sun. Cartographic skills were also improving and represented an ideal means of delineating the new knowledge.

At a most basic level, maps were required to record the physical presence of land and of physical features. In particular, information regarding safe havens was required and, as knowledge increased, so these charts developed into maritime charts detailing safe channels, expected water depths, hazards to navigation and so on. It is important to remember that at this time all trade was sea-borne and the vulnerable ships of the period were at the mercy of the harsh climate often to be encountered.

Out of discovery came possession and many of the maps that were produced from the colonial era were designed to show land ownership. On a global scale, these maps could illustrate the distribution of land between the great nation states, often as a result of a settlement after a war, or between the colonists and the native Americans. At a more local level, the maps could illustrate the ownership of parcels of land that had been divided between individual colonists. In the Eurocentric way in which North America was colonised, the great European monarchs granted huge areas of land to their subject for the creation of colonies; while these often took account of major geographical features, such as rivers, they were quite often arbitrary in the delineation of borders. The proprietors of these new provinces or colonies would then sub-divide these holdings for the settlers. At a time when there was no other title to the land, the precise delineation of holdings was critical. While, certainly in the early days, the more global representation of the region was suspect, the smaller the areas covered the greater the accuracy. There had been a long tradition of detailed estate maps in Europe, in particular among the abbeys and major land owners, and mapping of a small locality was, therefore, a skill widely practised.

Finally, from possession comes conflict. One of the major factors leading to the colonisation of the Americas was the prevailing belief in 'Mercantilism' — a belief that held that the world only possessed a fixed amount of wealth and that one country could only increase its own prosperity by grabbing wealth from another country. The vast opulence of the Americas — fostered both from the actual wealth brought back by the early explorers and by the myth of El Dorado — was to act as a magnet to European powers eager for their share of this new found prosperity. Initially many of the settlements established were in the form of trading posts, but it was inevitable that the conflicts — religious, political and economic — that dominated Europe in the 300 years from the discovery of the Americas through to the French defeat at Waterloo would have their echoes in the New World. Many of the maps illustrated in this book show fortifications, either actual or proposed, and campaigns. The military were among the most important map makers, with the skills and resources to undertake precise surveys. It is no accident that the United Kingdom's primary mapping agency has the name Ordnance Survey as it grew out of a department of the military.

The Development of Cartography

Since the fallof the Roman Empire, European culture had, to a significant extent, lost many of the skills and arts that the classical civilisations of Egypt, Greece and Rome had possessed. Among the skills that had disappeared during the so-called Dark Ages was cartography. The Greeks and Romans had had the skills and the knowledge to produce quite detailed maps which bore some resemblance to the actual landscape and topographical details; post-Rome, however, the civilisations of western Europe lacked the cartographers with the knowledge to undertake the work. Religion had a great deal to do with this. The famous Mappa Mundi on display at Hereford Cathedral in Britain was completed by Richard of Haldingham in the 13th century; this map, purporting to show the whole world, has at its centre Jerusalem reflecting the contemporary Christian belief that the earth was flat, the sky represented the heavens and that all centred on Jerusalem.

The Renaissance was a period of flowering in the arts and in literature. It was a period when scientific discoveries were being made and when mankind's knowledge of the world was increasing. Exploration, both by land and by sea, had expanded the knowledge of the earth and had undermined fatally the existing tenets. During the later Middle Ages, there was an increasing skill in cartography, just as there was in art, and this was initially reflected in local or district maps. These small scale maps were often the result of property disputes or of the major landowners, often the church, delineating their property.

At the start of the 15th century, the production of these local maps grew dramatically. To this was added the publication in 1406 of a map of the then known world produced by Ptolemy, a late Roman cartographer drawn in a style similar to that which we would recognise today. This map was widely circulated and in 1475 the first printed version appeared. With the arrival of printed maps, the skills of the cartographer — which previously had been limited to only a handful of people, many of them monks in the major monasteries — became more widely dispersed.

Just as the knowledge of cartography was increasing, so too were the skills associated with surveying. Although still rudimentary by modern-day standards, the principle of constructing maps by actual measurement was growing in importance. Units of measurement may have varied from country to country, even district to district, but the moment that maps became scaled so they became more useful to, for example, property owners and to mariners. The skills associated with the construction of detailed maps were also enhanced during the 16th century by the discovery of triangulation, the art by which the relative positions of places could be determined through the use of a precisely measured base line and detailed use of angles.

Thus, just at the time when European explorers were starting to investigate the New World, the skills and means were developing for them to record accurately, the land that they had found. For explorers of North America, however, there was a further layer of knowledge that they could call upon and that was the map-making tradition of the native population. There was a strong tradition of symbol maps amongst the Indian populations of both North and South America. Some of these were carved on stone, while others were much less permanent, being drawn on animal skins, on tree barks or in the sand. Many of the early maps produced by the explorers in the New World were able to draw upon these symbol maps which did not die with the arrival of the Europeans. The native population continued to use such methods well into the 19th century; as late as 1849, for example, Indians from the Chippewa tribe in Wisconsin sent a map to the then President of the of the United States — Zachary Taylor — as part of a petition. This map was produced from bark of a birch tree and illustrated the area in which they lived; each family was also identified, using the fish or animal that was the family's individual totem.

Many of the early cartographers of the 16th and 17th centuries were not specifically trained. Some — like Leonardo da Vinci — were artists and scientists interested in expanding human knowledge; others came from more mundane backgrounds. The great British cartographer John Speed, who flourished in the early 17th century, was a tailor by profession. A figure like Speed was able to develop as a cartographer without ever having visited the regions that he portrayed for two reasons. First, he was able to copy the work of earlier cartographers as the concept of copyright as we know it today did not exist. Second, this information could only come to him through the increasing availability of detailed prints produced by craftsman, many of whom came from the Low Countries (Belgium and Holland). This latter point is of note; these craftsman-printers were producing printing plates in languages in which they were not well versed. It was inevitable that place names would be mis-spelt and these errors would be perpetuated by those using the printed maps as sources for newer publications.

By the start of the 16th century, the skills required to produce detailed scale maps were in place. Many of the earliest drawn were produced by the military — for either offensive or defensive reasons — and the military were, as the maps in this book show, to maintain an important role in cartography right through to the modern age. Many of the scale maps produced still retain elements of the older tradition of pictorial representation. To cartographers in the Renaissance, and to those working today, the pictorial representation of buildings and other facilities helps to codify. The pictorial representations that are visible in many of the maps included in this selection have three effective roles: to decorate; to provide a useful symbol (for a church or house, for example); and, to form a foundation for other information.

About the Maps

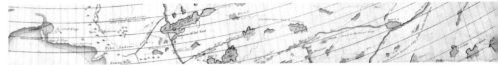

All the maps illustrated in this book have been drawn from the large collection held by the Public Record Office at Kew in west London. This is the major holding of all public documents in the United Kingdom. The maps are derived from three main government departments — the Foreign Office, the Colonial Office and the War Office — and reflect the interests and concerns at the time they were compiled. Although the majority of the maps were produced by English-speaking cartographers, the collection also includes numerous maps produced for other nations involved in the exploration and the exploitation of the New World. Even after the United Kingdom ceased to have dominion over the strategic interests, the original 'Thirteen Colonies', in particular with concerns over Canada and territorial disputes with the USA, meant that documentation covering the latter was collected through the 19th century and beyond.

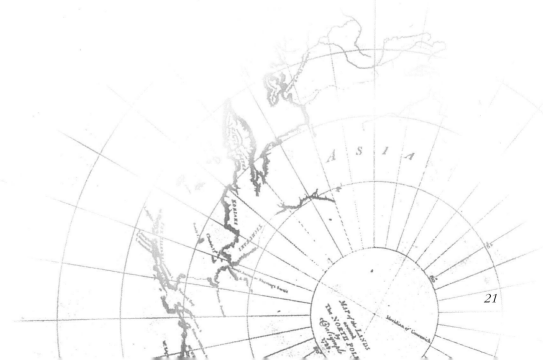

Virginia 1612

Left: This is one of the earliest maps covering the British interest in North America. It shows 'Virginia discovered and described by Captain John Smith'. The fact that this was very much *terra incognito* is illustrated by the fact that the boundary of known territory is indicated by an 'X' at the point reached. John Smith was one of the earliest of the English pioneers. He set sail in December 1606 with 104 men and boys on board three ships—the *Susan Constant*, the *Godspeed* and the *Discovery*. Thirty miles up the James River they established a base, which they called Jamestown after King James I. Unlike the earlier English settlement at Roanoke, which had failed at the end of the 16th century, Jamestown was to survive. The primary imperative for its establishment was trade, and the traffic was controlled by the Virginia Company in England—unprofitably until the development of the tobacco industry towards the end of the second decade of the 17th century. Powhatan (illustrated at left) was one of the local Indian leaders, best known as the father of Pocahontas, the Indian princess taken to London after having saved John Smith's life.

The Americas 1627

Below (detail) and Overleaf: Derived from John Speed's *America* published in 1627, this map shows 'America with those known parts in that unknown world both people and manner of building described and enlarged'. The inset drawings at the top show plans of Havana, San Domingo, Cartagena, Mexico City, Cuzco, Isle of Mocha (Chile), Rio de Janeiro and Olinda. John Speed was a tailor by profession, but was a skilled cartographer whose work in England was amongst the best at the time. Like numerous other contemporary cartographers, he would never have seen the areas that he was depicting, but taking advantage of the fact that there was no concept of copyright, used his skills to abstract material from other printed sources. Although the interior of the continent is fairly fanciful, the map is remarkably accurate as to the shape of North and South America, and of their relationship with the Caribbean islands. Note that California is still portrayed as an island, as it would be for a number of years yet, and that further exploration of the Western seaboard had still to be achieved.

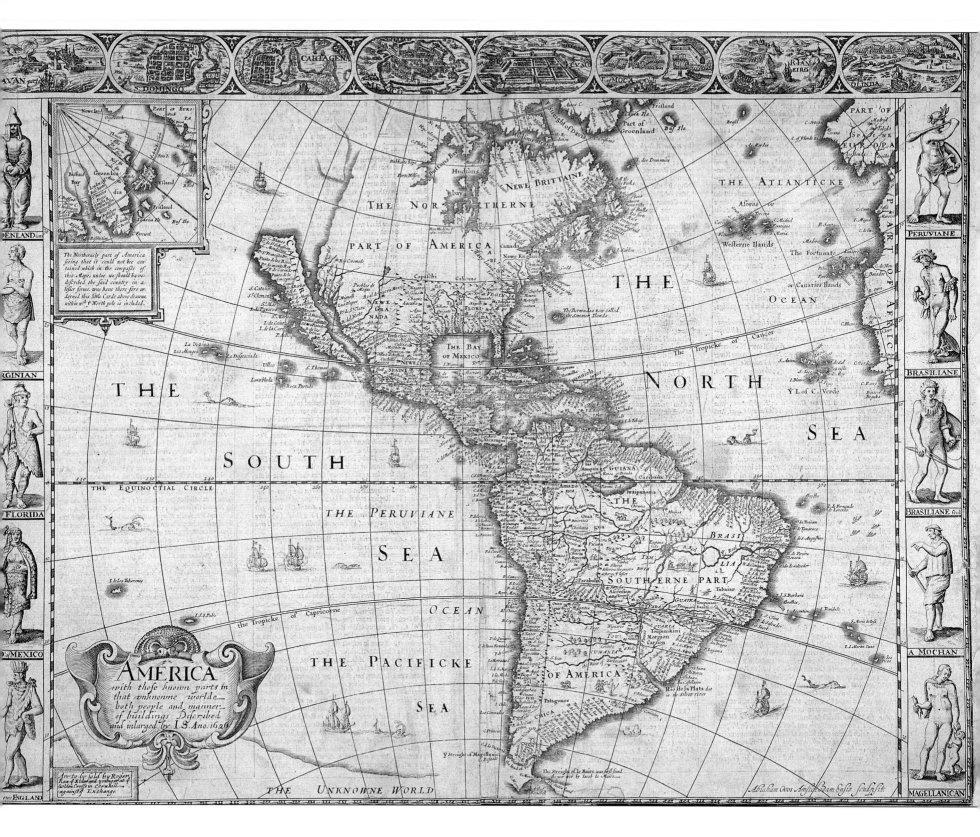

24

Septentrionalissimas Americæ partes, Groenlandiam puta, Islandiâ et adjacentes, quod Americæ tabulæ commodé comprehendi non potuerint, peculiari hac tabella Spectatoribus exhibendas duximus.

AMERICÆ
nova Tabula.
Auct: Guilielmo Blaeuw.

TERRA AUSTRALIS INCOGNITA.

AMERICA SEPTENTRIONALIS

AMERICA MERIDIONALIS

MAR DEL NORT

MAR DEL ZUR

OCEANUS

MARE PACIFICUM

Tropicus Caneri

Circulus Æquinoctialis

Tropicus Capricorni

Peruvianus

OCEANUS ATLANTICUS

EUROPÆ PARS

HISPANIA

AFRICA PARS

BRASILIA

POTOSI

CARTAGENA

St. DOMINGO

MEXICO

CUSCO

ISLA MOCHA in Chili

RIO IANEIRO

OLINDA in Pharnambuco

Groenlandi.

Virginiani.

et Regina Florida.

Iove Albionis Rex.

Mexicani.

Peruviani.

Brasiliani.

Brasiliani milites.

Insulani de la Moche in Chili

Freti Magellanici accolæ.

Cam privilegio decem annorum.

25

The Americas early 17th century

Page 25 and Right (details): An interesting comparison is afforded between the map of 1627 (page 24) and this one drawn by Guiljelmo [Willem] Blaeuw [Blaeu] at some date between 1616, when the Straits of Le Maire were discovered, and 1638, when Blaeuw died. This map is a fine early 17th century representation of the Americas, and their relationship with West Africa and Europe. The borders of the map are decorated with figures of native tribes to the left and right, whilst the top has inset maps showing places such as Havana, in Cuba, and Mexico. Willem Janszoon Blaeu (1571–1638) was one of the leading cartographers in Amsterdam in the early 16th century, whose two sons were also to become noted cartographers. Born in Alkmaar, he was trained as an astronomer by the noted Danish scientist Tycho Brahe, before setting himself up in business in 1599 as an instrument and globe maker. He started producing maps in the early 1600s, covering both Holland and the world. In 1605/6 he produced a marine atlas, *The Light of Navigation*, which was to be highly influential and passed into several languages and editions. He intended to produce a major series of maps featuring the known world, but this was a long-term project. In 1630 he published a 60-map atlas called *Atlantis Appendix* and followed this up in 1635 with the first two volumes of his world atlas. By the early 1630s, shortly before his death, he became Hydrographer of the Dutch East India Company.

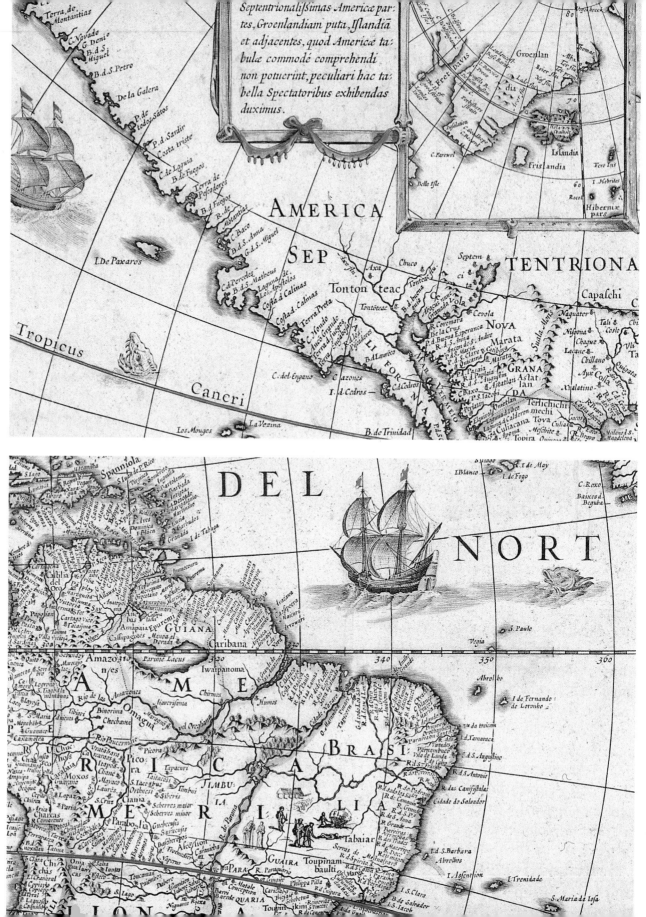

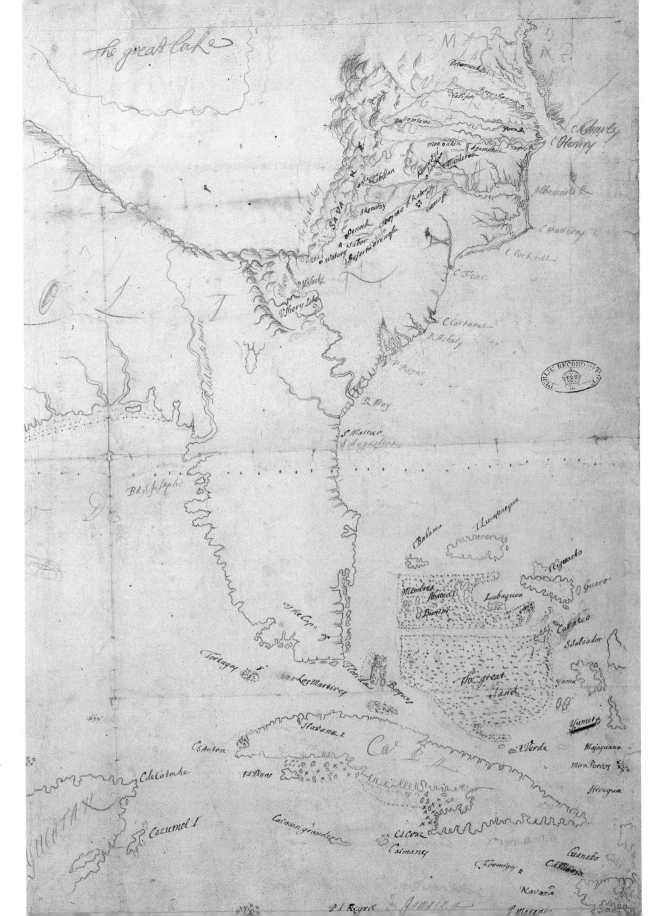

Mexico and Southern USA 1671

Left: This map shows the south-eastern part of the future United States, along with part of Mexico and Jamaica. It covers the eastern seaboard from Yucatan Bay to Chesapeake Bay and was drawn to an approximate scale of 96 miles to one inch. On the northern side there is a dotted line, roughly at about 29° North, which shows the southern limit of the Carolina grant. Carolina had been granted by King Charles II, the newly restored Stuart king on the British throne, on 24 March 1663 to Sir John Colleton. This charter covered the area between Virginia and the Spanish-controlled region of Florida.

27

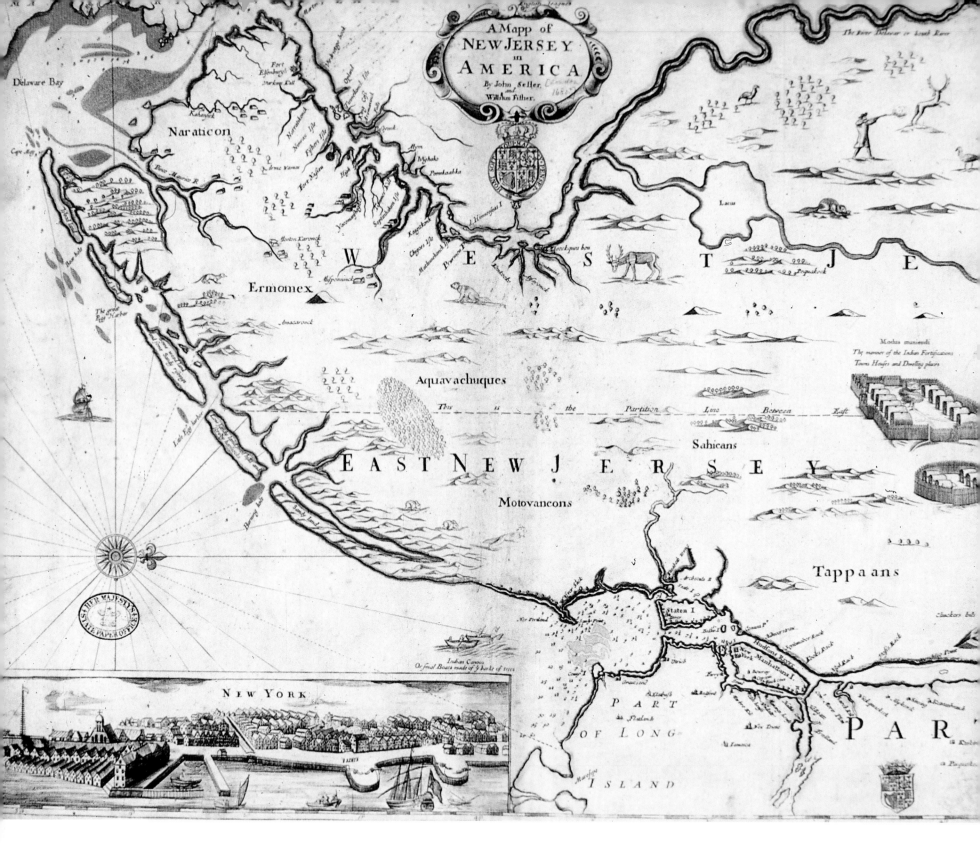

A Mapp of
NEW JERSEY
in
AMERICA
By John Seller
and
William Fisher.

Delaware Bay

Naraticon

Ermomex

W   E   S   T   J   E

Aquavachuques

Modus muniendi
The manner of the Indian Fortifications
Towns Houses and Dwelling places

This   is   the   Partition   Line   Between   East

EAST NEW J ERSEY

Sahicans

Motovancons

Tappaans

Clackers hook

NEW YORK

Staten I.

Indian Canoos
Or small Boats made of ye barke of trees

Hudsons River

New York Manhatans I.

PART
OF LONG

P A R

ISLAND

New Jersey c1680

Left: This is a map of New Jersey in America drawn towards the end of the 17th century by John Sellar and William Fisher. The map illustrates place names, rivers, soundings and also shows the hills in perspective. Also illustrated is a vignette of New York with its harbour viewed from the river. The state of New Jersey (or New Caeserea as it was also known for a period) was a proprietary creation established in 1664 under the patronage of Lord George Berkeley and Sir George Carteret. The same year was to see the British supplant the Dutch in New Amsterdam and New Netherlands, renaming the city and state 'New York'.

Connecticut 1698

Above right: Showing the boundaries of New Cambridge County in New England, this map is drawn to a scale of seven miles to one inch and shows the land as far west as the Connecticut River — effectively the present county of New London in the state of Connecticut. The estuary of the Connecticut River was fertile and was a draw for those settlers eager for land for cultivation. The colony was founded in 1635 by Puritans from the Bay Colony in Massachusetts under the leadership of Thomas Hooper. The resident tribe, the Pequot, was driven out in 1637. The Dutch also had an interest in the region; indeed, Hartford was originally the Dutch settlement of De Hoop, becoming New Hope when swallowed up by the British territory. Connecticut was granted its Colonial Charter by King Charles II in 1662.

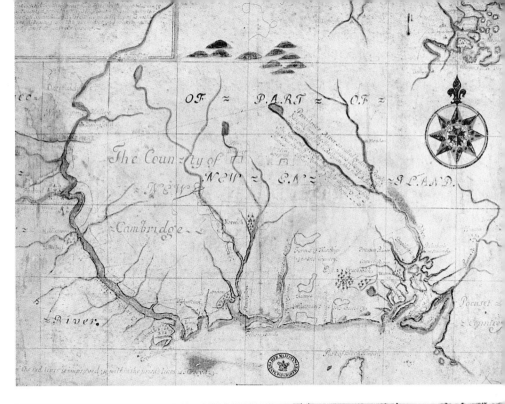

Maryland c1681

Below right: At a scale of approximately 10 miles to one inch, this shows the colonies of Maryland and Delaware with the adjacent parts of New Jersey and Virginia. Information given includes the counties, place names, rivers and creeks. More importantly, details of shoals and soundings are given, emphasising the fact that many of these early maps were an essential part of ensuring safe travel by waterway at a time when water represented the only reliable form of transport. The future colony of Maryland was founded as a refuge for persecuted Catholics by Sir George Calvert (later the first Lord Baltimore) and his son Cecilius. The Royal Charter, signed by King Charles I (who was sympathetic to the Catholics), was dated 30 June 1632 and the first settlers landed at a place they called St Mary's in 1634. The state was named Maryland in honour of Charles I's queen, Henrietta Maria. The Protestant/Catholic tension, which was such a mark of British history during the 17th century, was mirrored by events in Maryland and, after the Glorious Revolution of 1688 (which saw the last Stuart King, James II, overthrown), the Protestant residents petitioned the new King, William III, to make Maryland a royal colony; this happened in 1691 when as a result, as in Britain, Catholics were excluded from public office. The state, however, was restored to the control of the Calvert family in 1715, as the fourth Lord Baltimore had converted to the Protestant faith; it remained under the family's control until 1776. Delaware was first colonised from 1638 by Swedes, who established New Sweden on the Atlantic coast at Fort Christina (part of the area of contemporary Philadelphia). The Swedish presence was shortlived, the area passing to the control of the Dutch before the British took over after 1664. In 1682 what was then known as the 'Three Lower Counties' was bought by William Penn from the Duke of York and formed the basis of another Quaker establishment alongside Pennsylvania. Delaware was to be granted its own assembly in 1703 and was the first state, on 8 December 1787, to ratify the Constitution of the United States.

New York 1698

Far right: Described as 'Plan de la Ville d'Albanie dans le Province de la Nouvelle York en Amerique' (Plan of the town of Albany in the Province of New York in America), this plan shows Albany at the end of the 17th century. The initial impetus for the creation of many of the early European settlements in North America was trade, and in 1613 the Dutch sailed 150 miles up the Hudson River and created a new trading post. Initially, it was named 'Nassau', later becoming 'Orange' before finally becoming Albany. The creation of Nassau was part of the Dutch expansion in the region, which led in 1621 to the creation of the Dutch West India Company and the founding later in the decade of New Amsterdam (later New York). The region remained under Dutch control until 1664 when it was seized by the British and renamed. Albany is today the capital of New York State.

Right and Below (detail): The Province of New York in America and the territories adjacent, this map was drawn by Augustin Graham, Survey General, and was dedicated to the Earl of Bellomont, the Governor of New York, and to the Lords of the Council for Trade and Plantations. The northern part of the map is inaccurate and out of scale. In particular, Lake Champlain (Cortar's Lake) is shown northeast of the Hudson and not north.

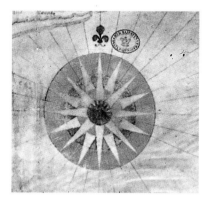

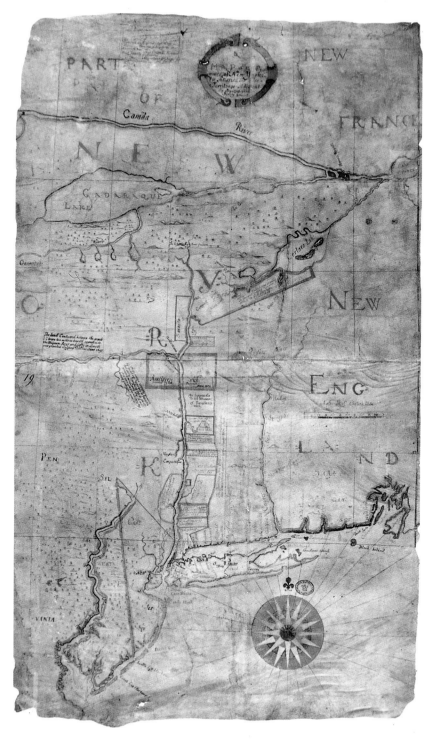

1. Citty Albania
2. The Kings Fort
3. The Wells the Fort
4. The Aquaduct that furnishes ye William ye Spring No 6
5. The Spring
6. The Fox kill
7. The Rutten kill
8. The Road to ye Half moon and Saratoge
9. The Protestant Church
10. The Towne house
11. Lutheran Church
12. North Gate
13. South Gate
14. East Gate
15. West Gate
16. Park Street Gate
17. Mr Livingston Gate
18. Scenectady Gate
19. Brick Kiln
20. The Tanner Houses
21. The Indian Houses
22. The Pasture
23. The Indian Prayer house
24. The Well upon the hill
25. Fishers Street
26. The old Dutch Fort

Boston 1699

Far right This map illustrates the defensive arrangements built upon Castle Island as part of the protection of Boston Harbour. They key describes in detail the actual buildings provided at the fort. The city of Boston was first settled in the mid-17th century and was named after Boston, in Lincolnshire, from where the early Puritan settlers had come. It became the capital of Massachusetts Bay province and, by the start of the 18th century, had become the largest English-speaking settlement in North America. During the 18th century, however, it was to be overtaken in population terms by both New York and Philadelphia.

Falmouth c1699

Centre right: Many of the place names adopted by the earliest settlers in North America reflected the places from which they had departed in the Old World. The initial settlers in what later became Maine came from the West Country of England, with the Plymouth Company being originally empowered to create one of the first English settlements in North America during the first decade of the 17th century. One of these settlements was Falmouth, named after the Cornish harbour. Like many of these early settlements, it required protection and this map shows what is described as the 'Old Fort'; note also the arrangement for the cannon demonstrating how rudimentary many of these early defences were. Although Maine was established relatively early, by this date it had fallen under the control of Massachusetts which had bought the state from the heirs of the founder in 1677. Maine was not to become an independent state until 1820 under the Missouri Compromise. Falmouth was to achieve an important footnote in history; it was in this town as well as Boston that small scale rioting took place after 1770 to prevent searches by customs officers. These riots were overlooked by the governor, Bernard, no doubt helping to sow the seeds of the future revolution. The town was burnt down by the British in 1775 as relations between the colonies and the British continued to deteriorate.

New Hampshire 1699

Above right and Right: Two views of Fort William and Mary situated on an island on the Piscataqua River in New Hampshire, dated 1699. The first part of the future colony of New Hampshire was granted to Sir Ferdinand Gorges in 1622, but was to be controlled by Massachusetts until it became a Royal Colony in its own right in 1677. The constant threat from both Indians and competing Europeans led to the construction of many of these strategic forts throughout North America. William and Mary came to the British throne in 1688 on the fall of James II and this fort must post-date their accession. Note that the Union Flag in both views only incorporates the red of the Cross of St George (for England) and the blue of the Cross of St Andrew (for Scotland); the flag familiar today only came into existence after the Act of Union with Ireland in 1801 when the additional red cross was included.

The Fort upon Great Island in Piscataqua River 1699

PLANATION ON THE PROSPECT DRAFT OF FORT WI

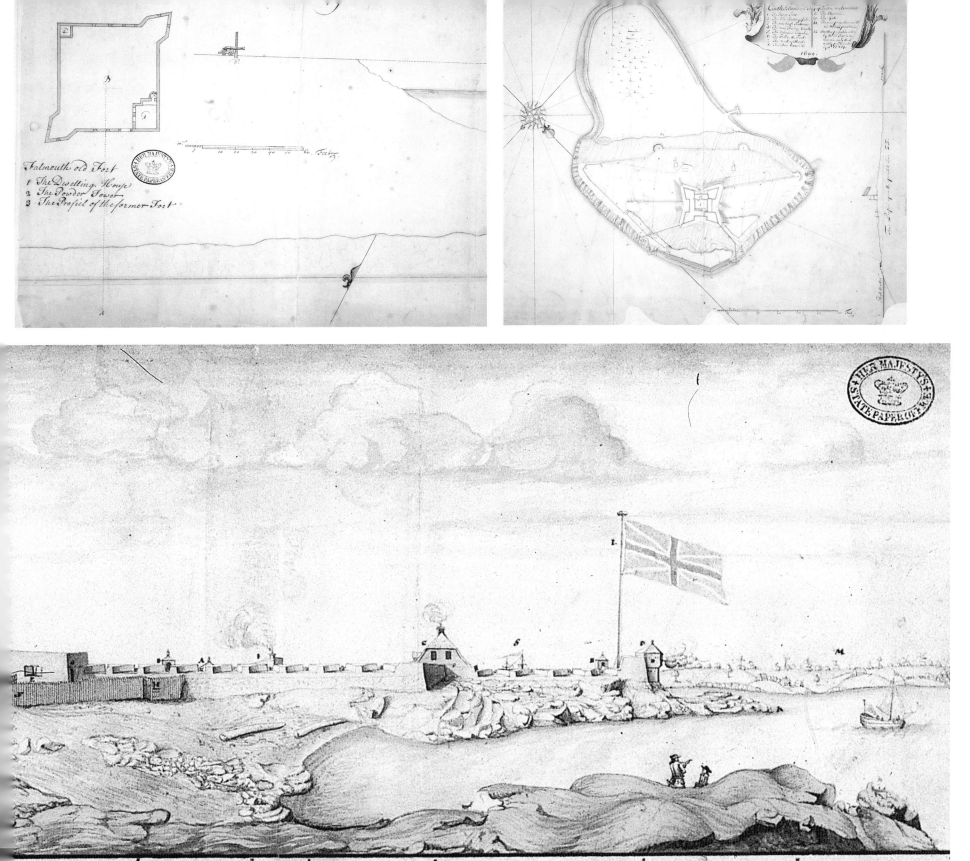

Falmouth old Fort

1. The Dwelling House
2. The Powder Tower
3. The Profil of the former Fort

Castle Island 1699

1 & MARY ON PISCATAQUA RIVER IN THE PROVINCE OF NEU-HAMPSHIR ON THE CONTINENT OF AMER[ICA]
mad Block house & Dongeon, E: Two new mad fresh Water Well, F: Watering place or a pype coming thre the Palisades for the QUEENS Ships to Water. G: The Sally port for to
qua River L: The new Flag Staff: M: Part of the Province of Main N: Justice Pepeill Garerson hous, O The Towne of New-Castle on the great Island. P. The Church. & The Minister hou[se]

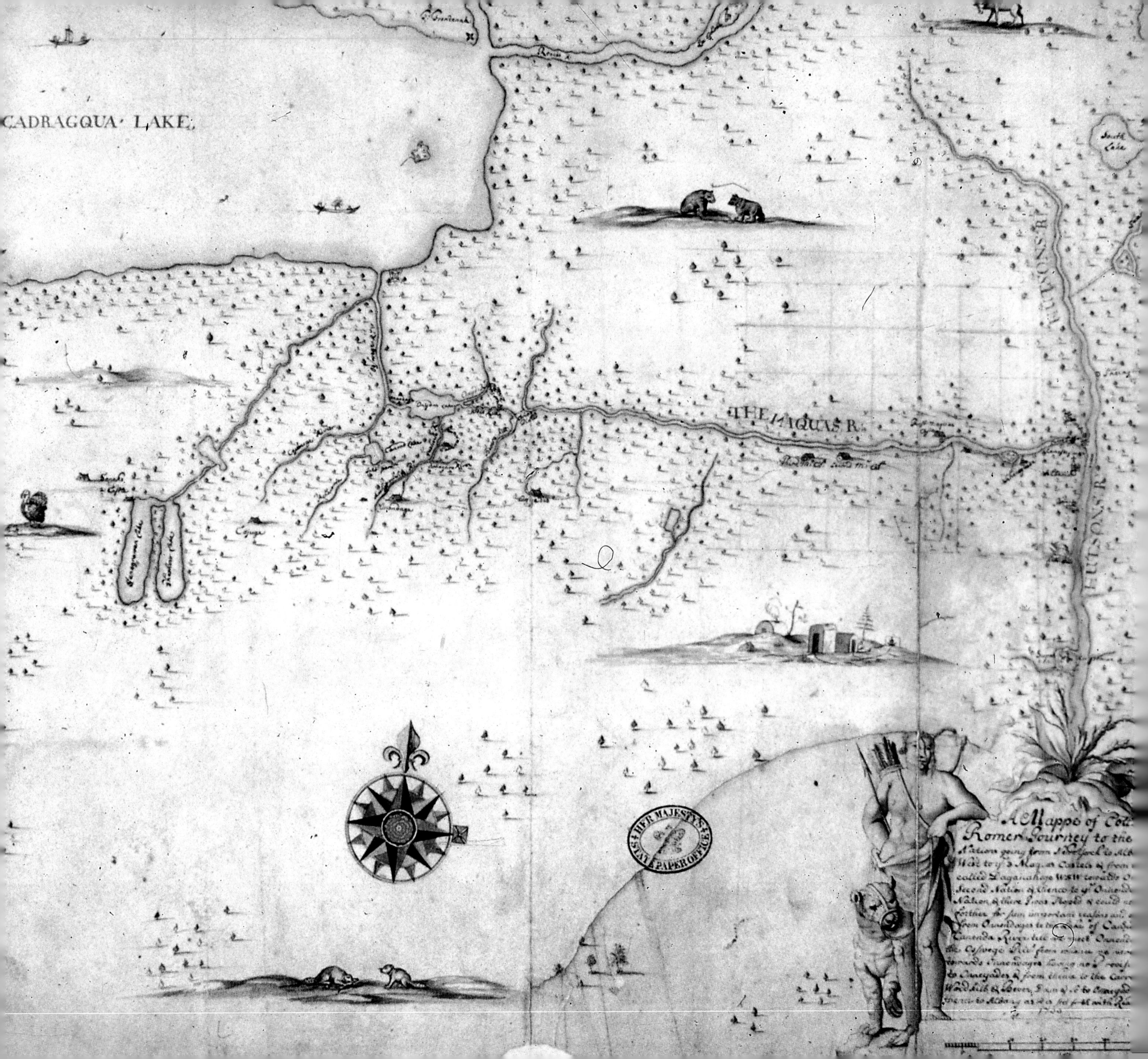

CADRAGQUA· LAKE

South Lake

HUDSONS R.

THE MAQUAS R.

Onondaga

Cayuga

HER MAJESTY'S
STATE PAPER OFFICE

A Mappe of Col:
Romers Journey to the
Nation going from...
Well to ye Maquas Castles...
called Paganahoge WSW...
Second Nation & thence to ye Oneyd...
Nation & there from Thence...
Further... from...
from Onondages to ye...
Cayenda River till ye Deck Onond...
the Cayuga Relation where...
towards Oneydages turning...
to Oneydades & from thence to the...
Windhill & Beever, than of it to...
thence to Albany as it is set...
1700

New York 1700

Left: This shows the journey of Col William Romer to the five Indian nations going from New York to Albany. The scale is 21 miles to one inch. The map also includes information on towns, Indian place names and encampments. The title cartouche gives full details of the actual journey, Romer describing it in the following terms: 'going from New York to Albany thence west to three Maquas Castles and from the last castle called Daganchoga west-south-westwards towards Onyades, a second nation, and thence to the Onnondayes, the third nation, and there I was stopped and could not proceed further for some important reasons and obliged to go from the Onnondayes to the lakes of Canenda down Canenda River till we meet Onnondayes River and the Ossiveger River from whence we were to return towards Ticonderoga having no provision and thence to the carring place and Bever Dam and so to Onyades again and thence to Albany'.

Above: This is described as a new map of the Hudson, or the North River, and was drawn by Col William Romer in 1700. At the centre is Staten Island, with Long Island and parts of New Jersey. Note the presence of a graveyard on Long Island and also the lack of development in this part of the future New York City. Staten Island is, today, one of the five boroughs that forms the city.

Pennsylvania 1700

Right and Below: Originally occupied by the Swedes in 1643 and later to become a Dutch colony, the area which was later to form the colony of Pennsylvania was seized by the British in 1664. In 1681 King Charles II granted the land to William Penn, a Quaker, and a large number of similarly minded people from Britain formed the initial population of the new colony. This map, dating from 1700, shows what is described as the 'improved part' — ie that which had been settled by Europeans — in Pennsylvania. The area has been carefully subdivided in parcels of land for the new settlers; note that those areas allocated to the 'proprietors' belong to the Penn family, who held 'proprietorship' of the colony until independence. The map was drawn by Tho[mas] Holme and was sold by P. Lea at the 'Atlas & Hercules' pub in Cheapside, London. It is dedicated to William Penn — 'Proprietor & Governor' — by John Harris. The map also includes as an inset the new city of Philadelphia, which is described as being two miles in length and one mile in breadth. Philadelphia, situated on the banks of the Delaware River, was founded in 1682 and by 1701 had a population of some 4,500. During the course of the 18th century, encouraged by the religious toleration of the colony, Philadelphia grew to become the biggest city in North America.

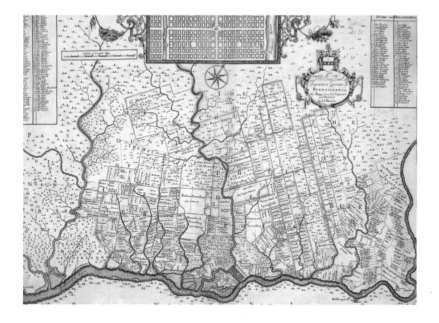

New England 1704

Right (details) and Far Right:
Described as 'A New Map of New England, New York, New Jersey Pensilvania [sic], Maryland and Virginia', this map was drawn by Robert Morden at the Atlas in Cornhill, and Phillip Lea at the Atlas & Hercules in the Poultry, both in London. It was sold by Thornton at the Platt in the Minories, also in London. The inset shows the approaches to New York and the whole map is decorated with ships, a whale hunt, various animals and other motifs. The original map was drawn to a scale of 21 miles to one inch, while the inset was to a scale of seven miles to one inch.

Robert Morden was one of the most influential of British cartographers in the late 17th century, until his death in 1703. He had premises in New Cheapside and Cornhill, in London, where, in addition to producing and selling maps, he also sold books and made globes and instruments. The date of the map is slightly imprecise, but the year 1704 is inscribed in pencil and it appears with this date in the official Colonial Office catalogue; given that Morden died in 1703, this date would seem to be a reasonable supposition.

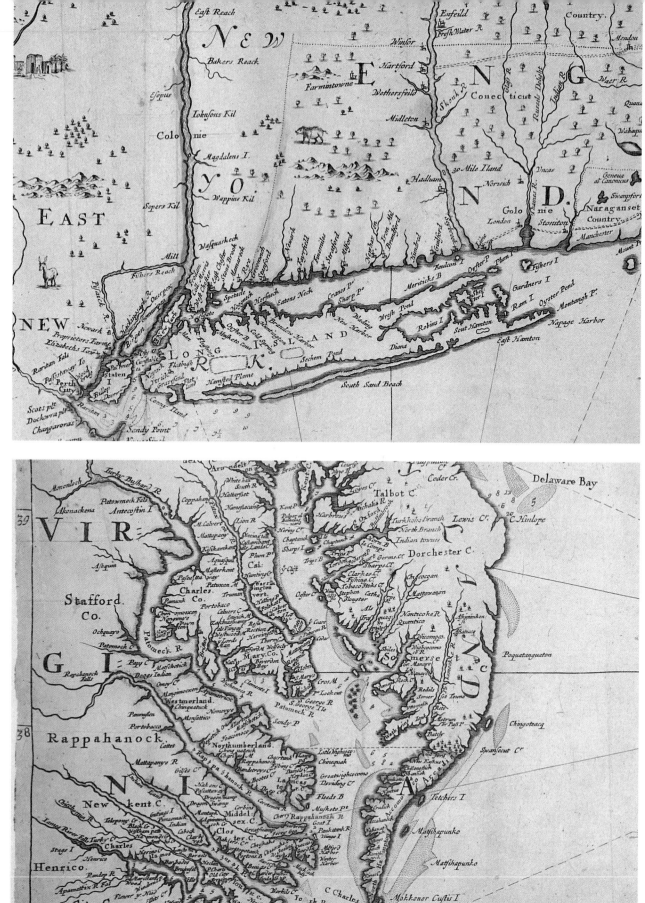

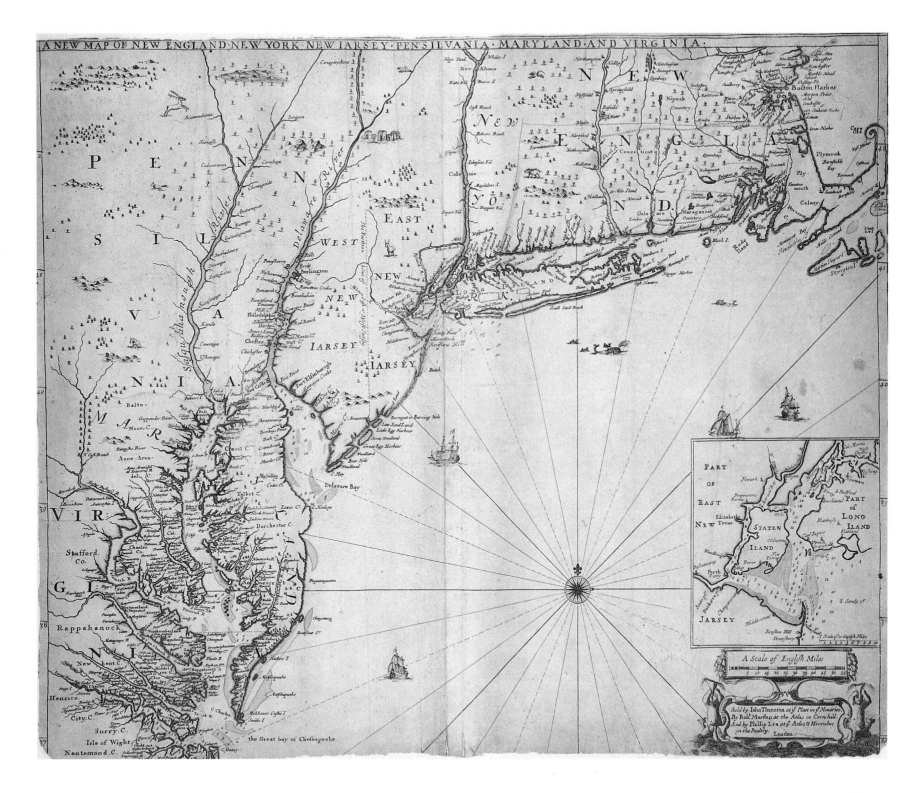

A NEW MAP OF NEW ENGLAND NEW YORK NEW IARSEY PEN'SILVANIA MARYLAND AND VIRGINIA.

N E W   E N G L A N D

N E W   Y O.R K

P E N N S I L V A N I A

NEW ENGLAND

EAST NEW IARSEY

WEST NEW IARSEY

Delaware Bay

M A R Y L A N D

V I R G I N I A

Rappahanock

Stafford Co.

Isle of Wight

Nantemond C.

the Great bay of Chesapeake

PART OF EAST NEW JERSEY

PART OF LONG ILAND

STATEN ILAND

A Scale of English Miles

Sold by Iohn Thornton at ye Platt in ye Minories.
By Robt. Morden at the Atlas in Corn-hill.
And by Phillip Lea at ye Atlas & Hercules
in the Poultry. London.

New Hampshire 1708

Right: This relatively crude map illustrates the region around the Piscataqua River in New Hampshire at the start of the 18th century. Pictograms are used to identify towns and individual buildings; at the estuary of the river can be seen Portsmouth. New Hampshire as a state was founded as a commercial enterprise by John Mason in 1623 and Portsmouth itself was first established in 1628, making it one of the earliest settlements to be permanently established by English colonists. By 1700, the population of the colony has been estimated at just under 5,000.

Carolina c1715

Far right, above: This map shows North and South Carolina, Florida and the Bahama Islands. Also illustrated is the disposition of the local Indian tribes along with the numbers of men in each tribe. At the bottom left is an inset which shows 'New France containing Canada, Louisiana etc in North America. According to the patent granted by the King of France to Monsieur Crozat dated 14 September 1712'. The first English settlement in North America, Sir Walter Raleigh's ill-fated Roanoke colony, was established off the future North Carolina in 1585. The development of the future states of North and South Carolina dates from the granting of a charter by King Charles II on 24 March 1663 to Sir John Colleton and seven others. Unlike other schemes, which envisaged emigration from Europe as the source of the new colonists, the proprietors of the Carolinas believed that they could encourage settlers from Virginia to the north. However, as so often, the initial plans proved over-optimistic and it was Anthony Ashley Cooper, later the Earl of Shaftesbury, who with the remaining proprietors, invested money to encourage settlers from Europe to travel to the region. A number of settlers also arrived from the island of Barbados, which was becoming over-settled by this time. The city of Charles Town (later Charleston) was founded in 1670. The proprietors retained control until 1719 — the last such arrangement in New England — and 10 years later, in 1729, separate administrations were established for North and South Carolina. It was North Carolina, on 12 May 1776, that became the first state to declare independence.

Florida 1722

Far right, below: This is inscribed as 'A copy of a draught of some places near the Mississippi'. It covers the coast from Santa Rosa Island to the Mississippi delta. It was received on 4 December 1722 from Mr Yonge who was then the agent for South Carolina. Among places that can be identified is Pensacola on the right; from its location on an inlet it is easy to see why this was regarded as one of the best natural harbours of the region. At the time the map was drafted, this area was under French control; the use of the French language is evidence that Yonge copied the map from an earlier French original.

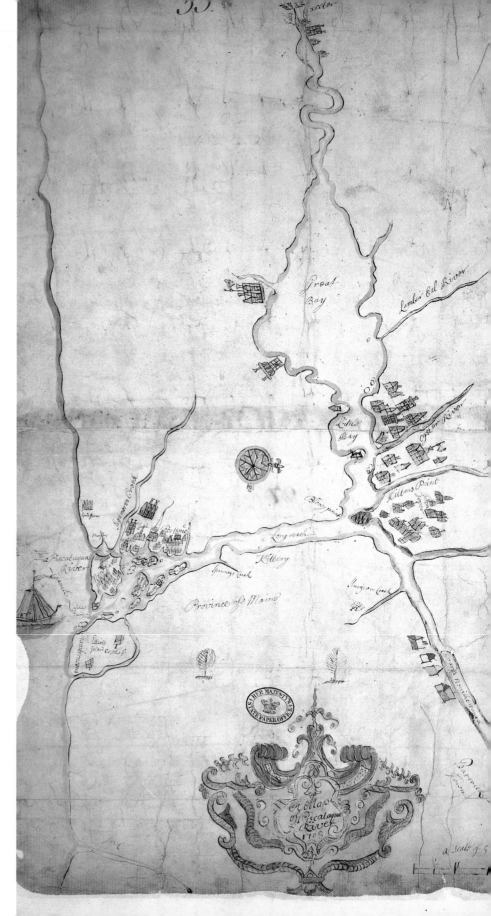

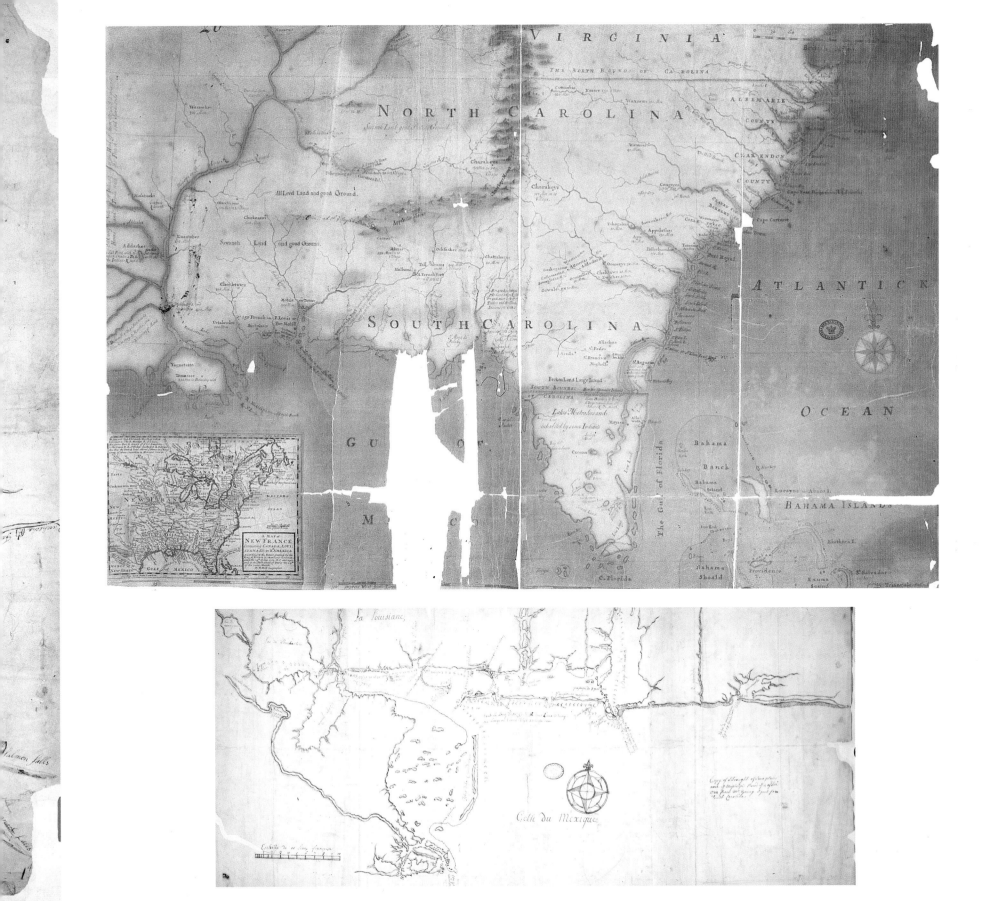

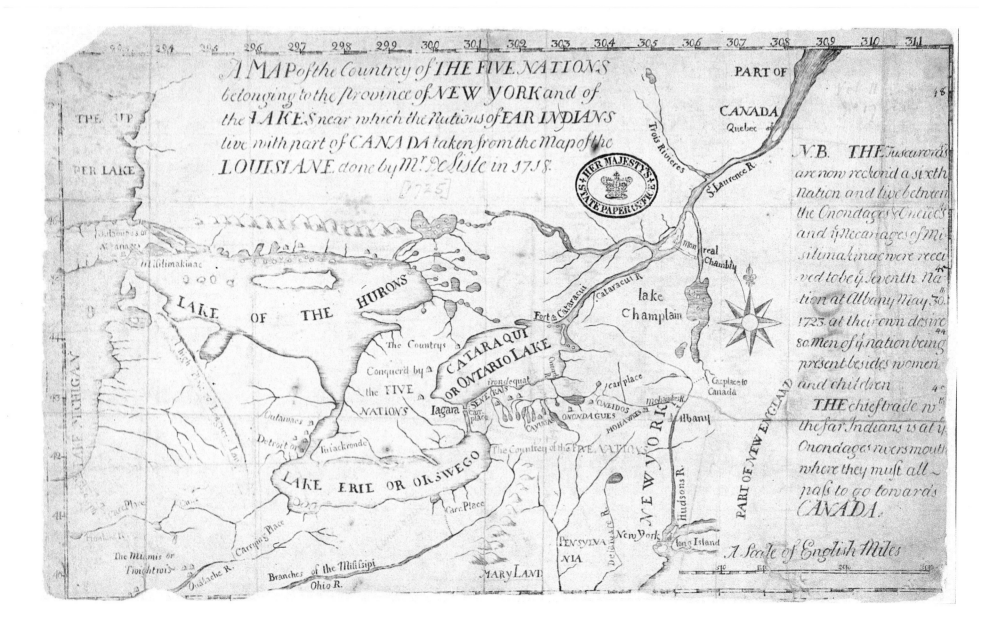

New York c1723-26

Above: This is described as 'A map of the country of the Five Nations belonging to the Province of New York and the Lakes near which the Nation of Far Indians live with part of Canada taken from the map of Louisiana done by Mr De Lisle in 1715'. This version was possibly produced by Cadwallader Colden, the Surveyor General of New York, as it appeared as the frontispiece for his book the *History of the Five Indian Nations of Canada*, which was published in 1747. Among the Indian tribes referred to in the notes accompanying the map are the Tuscaroras and the Necariages, who are described as the sixth and seventh nations.

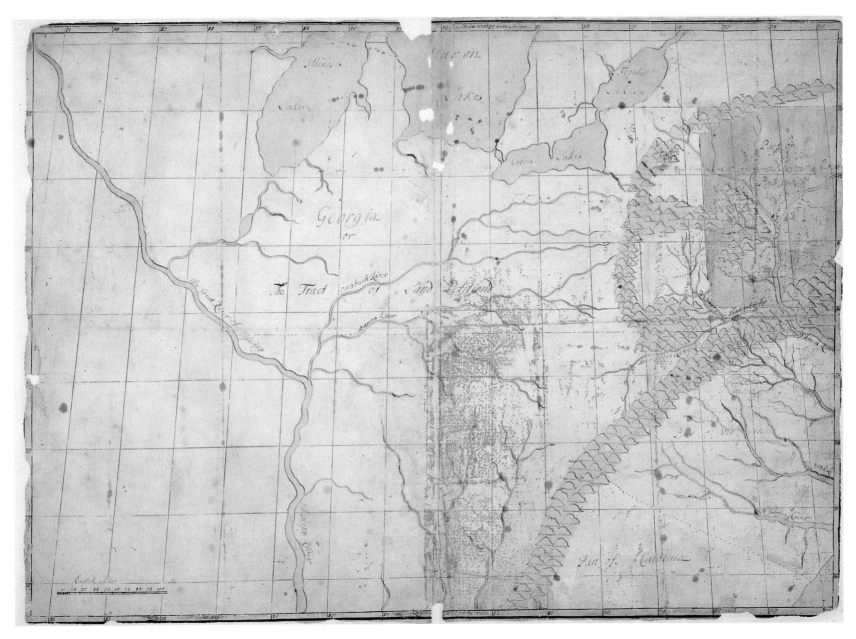

Eastern America 1731

Above: Covering Virginia as well as parts of Carolina and Pennsylvania, the Great Lakes and the Mississippi between latitudes 35° 40' and 44° North and longitudes 75° and 91° West, this map is endorsed 'Draught of a Tract of Land Petitioned for by Sir Wm [William] Keith and others'. Drawn to a scale of about 25 miles to one inch, the area being petitioned for lies mainly in the future states of Indiana and Ohio. The original of this map was received along with the Duke of Newcastle's letter to the British government on 3 August 1731. At this time, while the boundaries between the various English colonies themselves were largely determined, the western boundaries were less well defined. The area to the west of these colonies was the subject of territorial dispute between the British and the French and was to be the source of much conflict between the two European powers. The French had been the pioneering explorers of the region, with Sieur de la Salle being the first to travel to the future Indiana in 1679. The region was to be ceded to Britain at the Seven Years' War (1756–1763) and was then granted by Britain to the United States after the War of Independence. Petitions such as this were a common means by which ownership of land could be claimed on the part of colonists and settlers. The assumption was that, despite the presence of native tribes, the land was within the power of either the British or French monarch to grant to their subjects. After the United States achieved Independence, the western boundaries of the original colonies were regularised and land was ceded by the new states to create an area initially known as the 'Northwest Territory'; it was from this large region that the future states of Tennessee, Kentucky, Ohio, Indiana, etc, were to be created from 1792 onward.

Rhode Island 1736

Left: A map of the colony of Rhode Island. This was presented by the agent for Rhode Island in connection with the dispute between Rhode Island and Massachusetts. The map was compiled by Joseph Conant, surveyor of Windham County, Connecticut. The surveyor's oath and return, sworn before a Justice of the Peace, is written on the map. Separate from the map is a statement signed by the governor of Connecticut, Joseph Talcott, under the common seal of the colony, as to the authenticity of the surveyor's attestation. Founded in 1636 by Roger Williams, the colony of Rhode Island was established by religious dissenters from Massachusetts; it was the first British colony to recognise a difference between church and state and, as a result, became a haven for religious dissenters. It gained its Royal Charter in 1663. The local Indians, the Narragansett, were largely subjugated at the Great Swamp Fight in 1675. Much of the early history of Rhode Island is dominated by land disputes, both among its local citizens and with neighbouring colonies — as this map reveals. Rhode Island was to become the last of the original 'Thirteen Colonies' to ratify the consitution.

New Hampshire 1741

Right: A plan of the divisional boundaries between New Hampshire and the Massachusetts Bay (now Maine) from the Pigwakket River to the mouth of the Piscataque River. Drawn by Walter Bryant, a surveyor, of Newmarket, New Hampshire, this map is dated 16 April 1741 and has an oath from the surveyor attesting to the map's accuracy. Note also the comment 'A large swamp of white pine forest burnt by the Indians'. At this stage, New Hampshire was a separate colony but Maine was still part of Massachusetts and was to remain so until 1820. A map of this sort helps to emphasise that, while today the 'Thirteen Colonies' that made up British New England can be seen as an integral whole, at the time they were separate entities, each with territorial aspirations and differing attitudes. The unity that was to emerge after 1776 was a long drawn out affair and owed a great deal to mismanagement on the part of the British in the period after the War of Spanish Succession.

Charlottenbourg c1735

Left: The colony of Georgia was the last of the 'Thirteen Colonies' to be established. Founded in 1733 by James Oglethorpe both to prevent Spanish territorial acquisition north of Florida and as a charitable work — to facilitate the rehabilitation of those imprisoned for debt in Britain — Georgia was not an outstanding success initially, and in 1754 became a Crown Colony, when the proprietors reverted their rights to the King. This map shows the settlement of Charlottenbourg, with its churches, houses and obelisk, planned for the shores of the Altamaha River. Given the date, only a couple of years after the state's foundation, and the fact that Savannah itself was only founded by James Oglethorpe in 1735, this map probably portrays a scheme for development rather than an actual settlement. Like many of the original proprietors, Oglethorpe was over-ambitious for his new creation; in reality the European population of Georgia was only around the 5,000 mark in the mid-18th century.

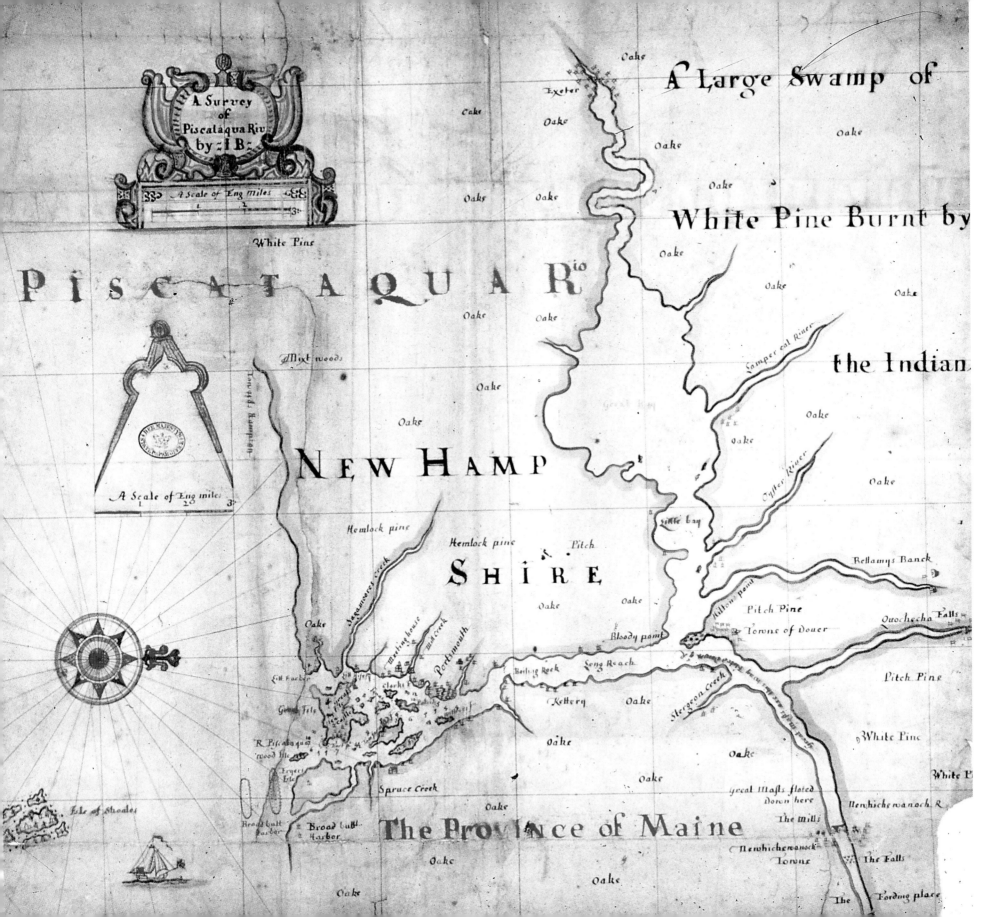

A Survey
of
Piscataqua Riu
by ˑI Bˑ

A Scale of Eng miles
1   2   3

White Pins

PISCATAQUA R.io

A Scale of Eng miles
1   2 3   3

Oake

Oake

Exeter

A Large Swamp of

Oake

Oake

Oake

White Pine Burnt by

Oake

Oake

Oake

Oake

Oake

the Indian

Lamper eal River

Mixt woods

Oake

Oake

Great Bay

Oake

Oake

Oake

Oake

NEW HAMP

Oyster River

Oake

Hemlock pine

little bay

Hemlock pine   Pitch

Bellamys Banck

SHIRE

Pitch Pine

Oake   Oake

Gilhon Point

Quochecha Falls

Sagamores creek

Towne of Douer

Bloody point

Washinghouse   mill creek

Pitch Pine

Hemlock pine

Boiling Rock   Long Reach

Fott Harbor

Portsmouth

Stergeon Creek

Kettery   Oake

clarki

Great Ile

Oake

R Piscataqua
wood Ile

Oake

White Pine

Fryers Ile

Oake

great Masts floted
Down here

Newhichewanock R

Spruce Creek

Oake

White P

Isle of Shoales

Broad butt
Harbor

Broad butt
Harbor

The Province of Maine

The Mills

Newhichewanock
Towne

Oake

The Falls

Oake

The   Fording place

Eastern America 1749

Right (details) and Far Right:
This is a map covering Pennsylvania (listed as 'Pensilvania'), New Jersey, New York and the three Delaware Counties. Also shown are adjacent parts of Maryland, Virginia and Connecticut and the map is embellished with drawings of two sailing ships. Drawn by Lewis Evans and engraved by L. Hebert, it was published by Lewis on 25 March 1749. Drawn to a scale of 15 miles to one inch the map also includes several paragraphs of remarks on the country and a paragraph of acknowledgements for the use of other surveys. Also of note is the table of distances between various important cities of the period. Although copying of maps by other cartographers was commonplace at the time — the concept of copyright was virtually unknown — acknowledgement was rare. One of the results of copying was that errors of spelling could easily appear, particularly if the original cartographer (as was often the case) was a non-native of the region being portrayed, and this error could be, therefore, perpetuated through the work of subsequent cartographers.

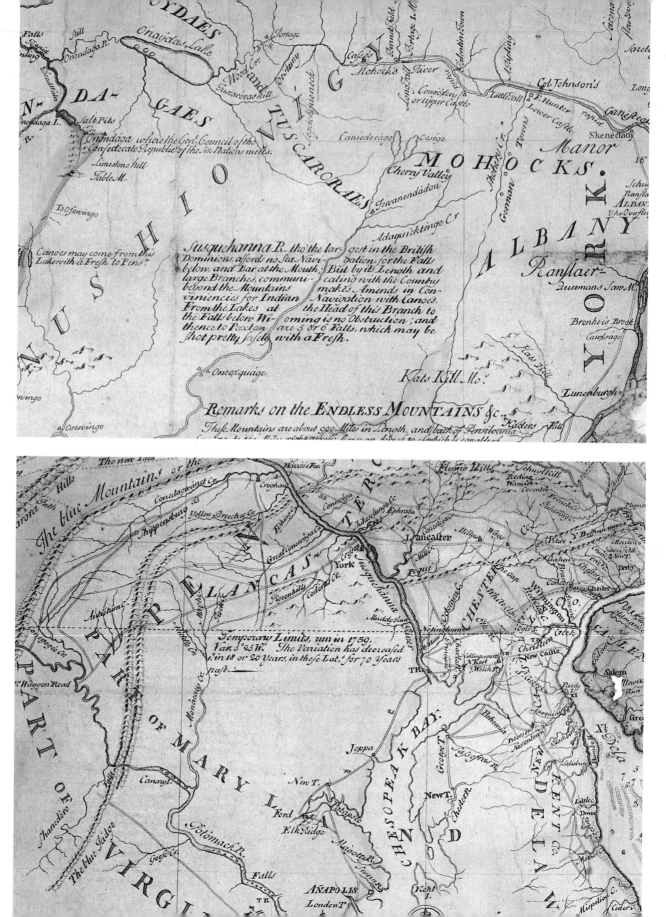

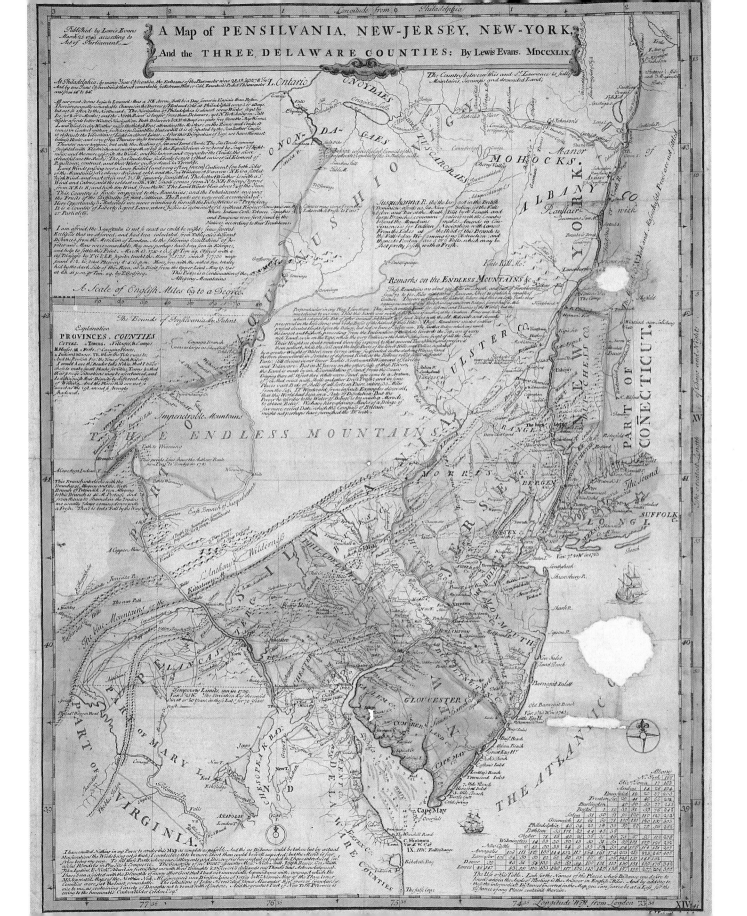

A Map of PENSILVANIA, NEW-JERSEY, NEW-YORK, And the THREE DELAWARE COUNTIES: By Lewis Evans. MDCCXLIX.

47

Louisiana 1752

Right (details) and Far Right: For much of the 18th century, as British and French influence grew, so the region to the west of the British Thirteen Colonies became a source of increasing tension between the two leading European powers. This map, dated to 1752, drawn by Eman Bowen to a scale of about 132 miles to one inch, is described as 'A New & Accurate Map of Louisiana, with Parts of Florida and Canada, and the Adjacent Counties. Drawn from Surveys, assisted by the most approved English & French Maps'. Of particular note with this map is the identification of specific regions with individual native tribes. By the early 1750s, the ongoing tension between Britain and France in this region was already developing into localised warfare. As a result of the War of Austrian Succession, which had seen Britain reinforce its position in Canada, the French decided to strengthen their position to the west of New England and in the early 1750s seized control of the Ohio Valley, building forts at the same time. While in Europe an uneasy peace existed between Britain and France, in North America the British decided to take unilateral action against the French with the result that British and Colonial forces, with the young George Washington to the fore, undertook a number of military actions in 1754 and 1755. Whilst these were not successful, they paved the way to the much more significant conflict represented by the Seven Years' War.

A NEW & ACCURATE
MAP of
LOUISIANA,
with Part of
FLORIDA and CANADA,
and the Adjacent Countries.
Drawn from Surveys,
assisted by the most approved
English & French Maps &
Charts.
The whole being regulated by
Astronl. Observations.
By Eman. Bowen.

English and French Leagues 20 to a Degree.

We think it proper to Inform ye curious
Reader, that in laying down ye Coast &
Boundaries of ye British Empire in
America, as well as that of Louisiana
Canada or New France Recourse
has been had to all ye Surveys & most
Authentick Charts & Maps hitherto
Published; But more particularly,
to Monsr. Bellin's Maps of Canada Louisiana &c drawn by him
for ye Use of P. Charlevoix's
History of New France; and
as our Maps of these parts, dif-
fer considerably from most
others, this difference must be
principally attributed to our re-
lying on Monsr. Bellin's
Authority.

SUPERIOR L.

HURON L.

MICHIGAN L.

ERIE LAKE

FRONTENAC
or ONTARIO L.

COUNTRY OF
TEMISCAMING

COUNTRY OF
NIPISSING

Temiscaming
Lake

Nipissing Lake

Quebec

COUNTRY
OF THE
PANIS

COUNTRY
of the
APACHES
and the
PADOUCAS

COUNTRY of the OSAYES

COUNTRY of the CHOUANONS

and the
CHEROKEES

COUNTRY OF
THE CENYS

MEXICO

NEW

LOUISIANA

FLORIDA

GEORGIA

CAROLINA

VIRGINIA

MARYLAND

PENSILVANIA

NEW JERSEY

NEW YORK

NEW ENGLAND

Long Island

Philadelphia

Delaware Bay

Cape Charles
Cape Henry

Currituck Inlet

Albemarle Sound

Hatteras Inlet
Ocacock Inlet

Cape Lookout

Cape Fear

Cape Carteret

Charles Town
Pt Royal

St Augustin
Matanca I.

Cape Canaveral

Mouths of the
Mississipi

Bay St Louis or
St Bernard

GULF OF MEXICO

ATLANTIC

OCEAN

West Longitude from London.

British North America 1755

Right and details to page 56:
'A map of the British colonies in North America with the roads, distances, limits and extent of the settlements, humbly inscribed to the Right Honourable the Earl of Halifax and the other right honourable the Lords Commissioners for Trade and Plantations.' This series of highly detailed maps was produced at a time when British power in the 'Thirteen Colonies' was probably at its height. Prior to the war of 1756-63, while there were disputes between colonies and colonial masters, these were very low key in comparison to those which occurred after 1763. There are a number of annotations to the maps, which help to emphasise how the boundaries between various of the colonies were still not finalised. One comment reads: 'The boundary of North and South Carolina is not yet settled: we have run a line between them only to give the public a view of those two colonies. The same is to be understood of South Carolina and Georgia.'

Another indication of this comes with the following: 'The bounds of Pennsylvania and Maryland and the Delaware counties are here laid down according to the late decree in Chancery [an English court] which is not supposed otherwise to affect the claims of any'; this was the territorial division settled by the Mason-Dixon Line in 1763-67. The extent of exploration is also clear in another comment: 'The head of the Mississippi is not yet known: it is supposed to arise about the 50th degree of latitude, and western bounds of this map beyond which North American extends nigh as far westward as it does to the eastward by all accounts.'

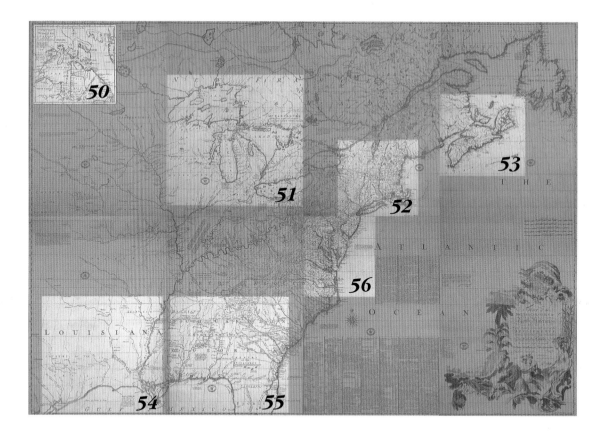

Above: Light areas in this composite map indicate sections which are displayed on the following pages.

Kiohicans   Red   River

Nadsoos   Salt House

Ouainco   Caligoa
Nassonites   Extent of Soto's
Cadodaquis   march from Florida

AKANSAS

French Fr. highest Settlem[?]   Kapp

Cahinoa   Sotouis   Lit: Akansas

Panima   Old   Ka[?]
Akansa's   Here Ferdinand[?]
                           first discover'd th[?]
French Fr[?]   Mississipi in 154[?]
          Ouyape
          550 miles up the M[?]

LOUISIANA

Riv: Rouge   Yatachez   Black   Ox River   River Mississipi

Salt Lakes   or. Point Coupee

Nacachez   River of the[?]
Natchitoches   The Indians on thi[?]
                                                 more in Alians[?]
                                                 English, for[?]
                                                 been dea[?]

Ofogoulas
Yasous
destroy'd
370 m[?]

COUNTRY   OF   THE

Nacanne   Isles and Lakes of the
          Nadaco   Adayes
Quiches   Bayou
          Assinais   Natchitoches   F. Rosalie
Mondaque   Ayches   Nauchees extirpated by t[?]
          Cenis   Naouadiches   Barbe   Ainais   French in 1730
Road   to   St.   200 m.
          Mexico   and   Mines of
                    Tayas   R.Ouidadets[?]
                                                              Avoyelles
          Bidaye   226 m. from the Sea
                                                                        St.Reine   Tonicas
Matigne   Pt. Coupee   Amit R.
   or   R. Flores   Ox R.
      Sabloniere   Mexican River   Chetimachas
Cinir R.   WANDRING   SAVAGE   INDIANS   Plaborninos R.
                    Trinidad River   Lake Pontchartrain
                              Madelame River   R.   NEW ORLEANS
                                                                                        Ouachas
          Judosa   Ascension Bay
                                        North Cape
                    Bounds of Carolina by Charter

Here Mr. La Salle
was kill'd in 1687

CENIS

St. Louis
   or
B. St. Bernard

La Salle settled,
discovering the

Depths of ye Mississipi
18 feet Water into Balise
12 feet over the Bar
45 feet within
50, 60 and 100 fathom after-
wards; and very deep, but rapid to the Illinois, counted 1200
Miles by water, and 770 Miles
in a Strait Line.

MOUTHS of the MIS[?]
South West Pass[?]

GULF   OF

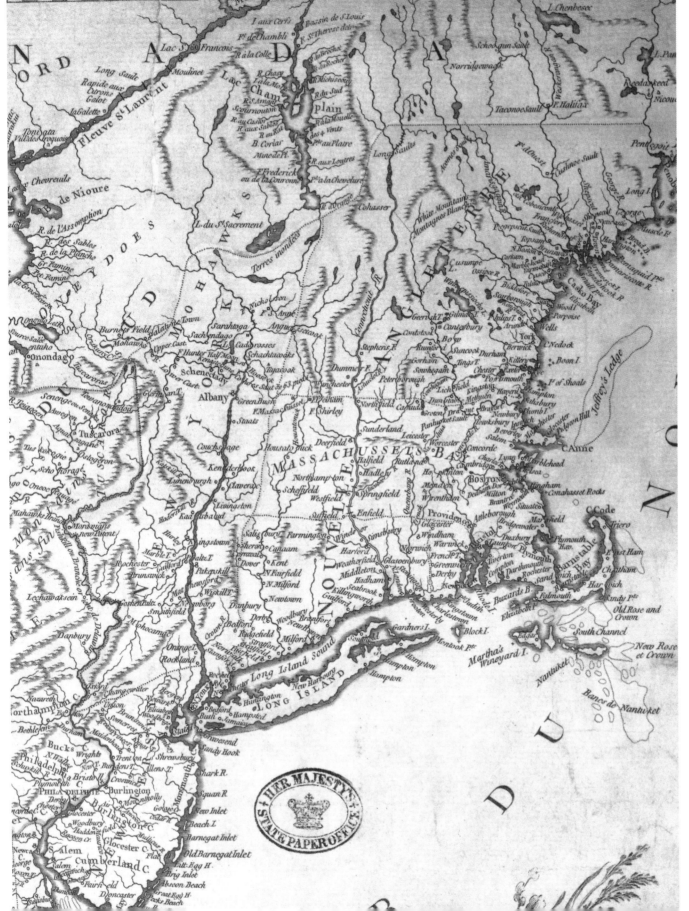

North America 1755

Left: Produced in France by Robert de Vaugondy, geographer to the King of France (then Louis XV), this map, with its legend in French, is significant as it shows the northern part of the French territories in North America at the time when British-French conflict in the region was starting to forge the destiny of both Canada and the future mid-west of the United States. The emphasis upon the course of the Ohio River is interesting as it was French ambition in this area, designed to prevent a British occupation, that led to into border warfare between the British and French settlers. The British colonies are well delineated, with the numerous settlements named. This map is ideal for showing two of the fundamental factors in the eventual French loss of its North American territories. First, since these were situated in land along the course of various waterways (the St Lawrence, the Mississippi, etc), resupply was dependent upon access to these rivers; during the war of 1756-1763, the British successfully blocked the St Lawrence and thus reduced the French ability to resupply the Canadian towns. Secondly, the density and scale of the British colonisation was much more intense than the French. To France, North America represented little more than a trading asset, to the British, with two centuries of religious strife behind it, North America represented a new beginning for huge numbers of émigrés.

Charlestown 1755

Left: This is a plan of a project to fortify Charlestown in South Carolina. It was undertaken by William de Brahm, Captain Engineer in the service of Emperor Charles VII (who ruled the Holy Roman Empire from 1742 to 1745, the only non-Hapsburg to do so), on behalf of the governor. The first Charles Town, established in 1670, was named in honour of the newly restored King Charles II and was sited on the banks of the Ashley River. This location proved unsuitable and the settlement moved to the peninsula where is situated as 'Charleston' today. The town grew to become an important trading station and at the time of the Revolution it was probably the wealthiest in the southern colonies. It was held during the War of Independence by British forces from 1780 until December 1781. The proposals for the construction of a fort at this time was a reflection of the growing British-French antagonism in the region.

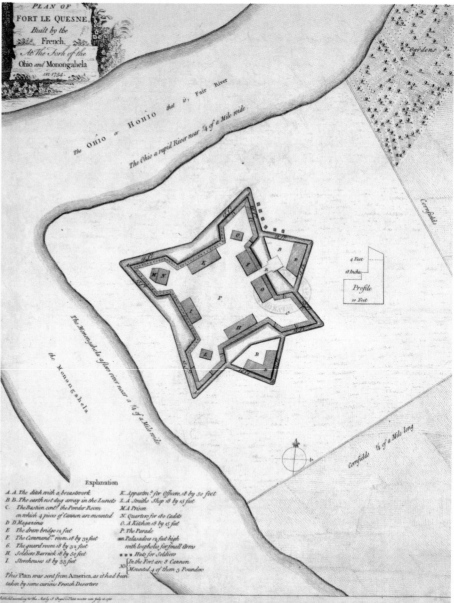

Fort Duquesne 1755

Right: This is a plan of the fort built at the fork of the Ohio and Monongohela rivers by the French in 1754; although labelled 'Le Quesne', the map actually illustrates Fort Duquesne, which is close to the site of the modern Pittsburgh. It was published in London, by J. Payne of Patternoster Row, on 15 July 1755. The diagram is annotated with the cryptic note 'This plan was sent from America as it had been taken by some curious French deserters.' Detailed information is included about the defences of the fort. Although there was officially peace between Britain and France after the War of Austrian Succession (1743-48), in the colonies there continued to be strife between the competing Europeans. In the early 1750s, the French decided to seize control of the Ohio Valley, in order to prevent further British expansion, and built a number of forts, including Duquesne, to safeguard their position. In 1754, the Virginians, under the command of George Washington, sought to dislodge the French, but were soundly beaten in July of that year. It was in response to this defeat that further military action occurred the following year, with the British Colonial forces led by General Edward Braddock. One consequence of the 1754 defeat was the realisation, inspired by Benjamin Franklin, that individual states could not take on the French single-handed; the result was his bold Albany Plan, which envisaged the colonists acting together. Although this was ultimately unsuccessful, it did lead conceptually to the United States in due course.

Massachusetts 1755

Right and Below: Published on 29 November 1755 by Thomas Jefferys at Charing Cross, London, this map shows the provinces of Massachusetts and New Hampshire, along with the colonies of Connecticut (spelt as 'Konektikut') and Rhode Island. Note that the future state of Maine, which at this time was under the control of Massachusetts, is described as 'Eastern Massachusetts'. The map also includes detailed insets of the harbour at Boston and Fort Frederick at Crown Point.

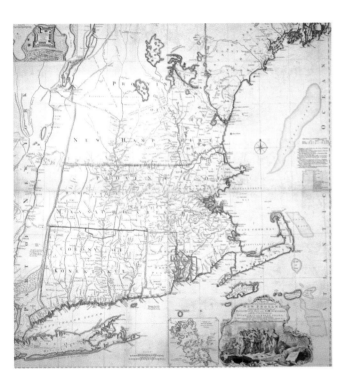

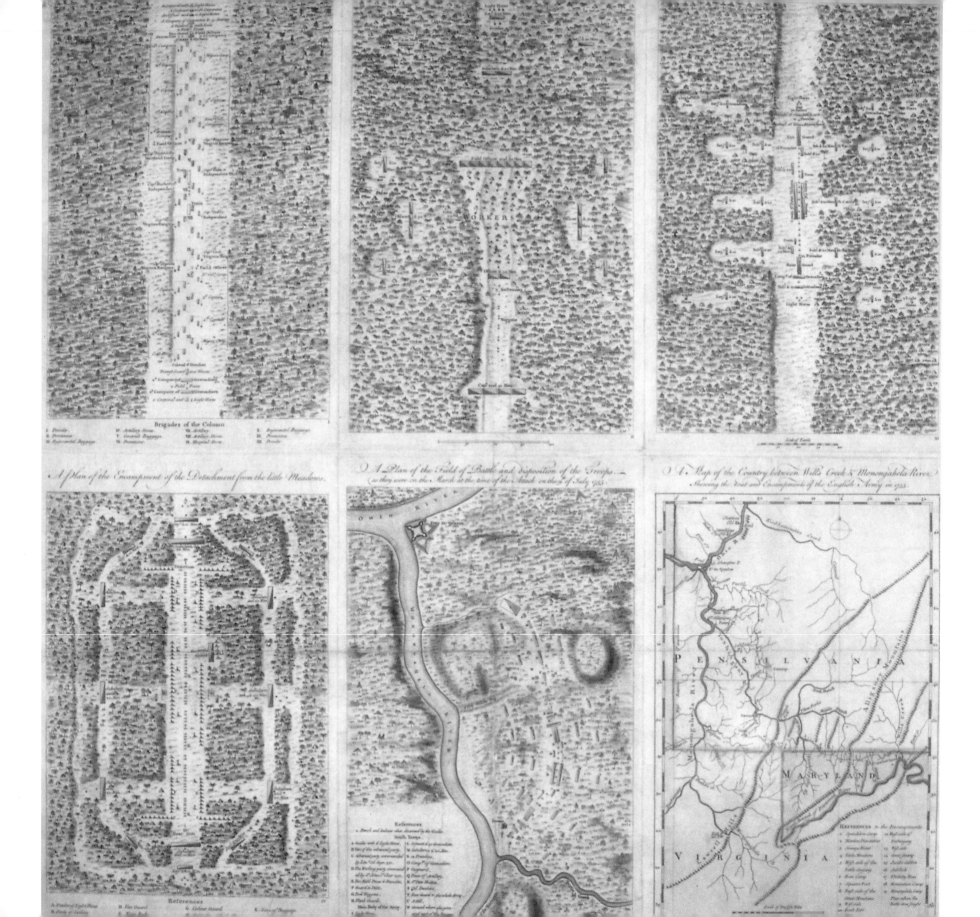

Brigades of the Column

A plan of the Encampment of the Detachment from the little Meadows.

A Plan of the Field of Battle and disposition of the Troops as they were on the March at the time of the Attack on the 9 of July 1755.

A Map of the Country between Wills Creek & Monongahela River Shewing the Rout and Encampments of the English Army in 1755.

OHIO RIVER

PENSILVANIA

MARYLAND

VIRGINIA

Pennsylvania 1755

Left: This sequence of six maps, published in Jeffery's *A General Topography of North America and the West Indies* in 1768, shows the ill-fated campaign waged by General Edward Braddock against the French in 1755. The six maps illustrate the following:

1. The line of March with baggage;
2. The disposition of the advanced party of 400 men;
3. The line of march of the detachment;
4. Encampment of the detachment;
5. Plan of the field of Battle at Fort Duquesne on 9 July 1755;
6. Map of the country between Will's Creek and Monongahela River showing the route and camps of the English army in 1755.

Braddock's campaign was an extension of European warfare into the Americas. His army comprised 1,400 redcoats and 450 'blues'; the latter were provincial soldiers recruited locally and included two figures who were to have a major influence on later American history — George Washington and Daniel Boone. The campaign was a disaster for the British forces; Braddock ignored warnings and marched his army into an ambush. Most of the British forces, including Braddock himself, were killed; Boone escaped and was also to serve with the British forces that avenged the defeat in 1758. Following the British victory in 1758, a new base — Fort Pitt (named after the then British Prime Minister and today known as Pittsburgh) — was established.

Maine 1755

Right and Below: Published by Andrew Miller, of the Strand in London, on 14 May 1755, this map shows the province of Maine, Originally drawn by Thomas England in 1754 an inset shows the region round Quebec produced by a French deserter in the same year. The map is dedicated to the then governor of the Massachusetts Bay province, William Shirley. Apart from the inset covering the Quebec region, other insets show three settlement: Frankfort, built by the Plymouth Company in 1752; Fort Halifax, built by the Massachusetts Bay government in 1754; and Fort Frederick at Crown Point built by the French in 1731. Maine had become part of Massachusetts Bay in 1691 and was to remain so until it was separated to become the 23rd state on 15 March 1820. The northernmost boundary of the state of Maine, effectively covered by the inset showing the Quebec region, was not finalised until an agreement with Britain in 1842.

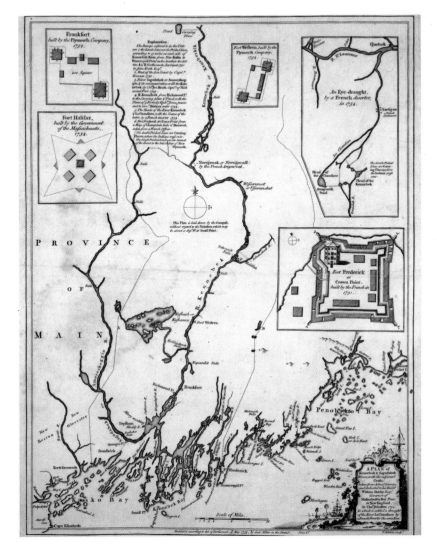

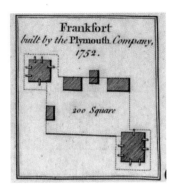

Philadelphia c1755

Right: This dramatic perspective shows the east prospect of the city of Philadelphia. It was drawn by George Heap from the Jersey shore under the direction of Nicholas Skull, who was the Surveyor General of the Province of Pennsylvania. In addition to the prospect, the map also shows a street layout as well as a view of the state house and the battery with union flag. The primary view has a key to identify certain major buildings: 1 = Christ Church; 2 = state house; 3 = academy; 4 = Presbyterian church; 5 = Dutch Calvinist church; 6 = the court house; 7 = Quaker Meeting House; 8 = High Street wharf; 9 = Mulberry Street; 10 = Sassafras Street; 11 = Vine Street; 12 = Chestnut Street; 13 = drawbridge; and 14 = cornmill. The map was published by T. Jefferys at Charing Cross in London. The city of Philadelphia was founded in 1682 and by the start of the 18th century had become a flourishing commercial centre. Not only did the trade to and from Pennsylvania pass through the city, but it also served Delaware, the lower part of New Jersey and Maryland. By 1760, shortly after the date of this drawing, Philadelphia had a population in excess of 23,000 — by the eve of the revolution it had reached more than 40,000. This made the city the largest in the North American colonies and one of the largest cities in the British Empire; it was probably only exceeded by London, Edinburgh and Dublin. The city, with its more liberal attitudes, was also to be home to Benjamin Franklin (1706-90), who moved to Philadelphia from Boston, and was highly influential in public affairs and politics.

An EAST PROSPECT of the CITY of PHILADELPHIA; taken by Geo

A DESCRIPTION OF

PHILADELPHIA, the Capital of Pennsylvania, is situate on the West side of the River Delaware, on a high and pleasant Plain, the City is laid out in form of an Oblong, two Miles in length, and one in breadth, bounded on the East by Delaware River, and on the West by the River Schuylkill, the Streets are all strait and parallel to the sides of the plan, and consequently cut each other at right Angles, none of which are less than 50 and the widest 100 feet in breadth, their Houses are built with Brick, and are from two to three and four Stories high; the Buildings are extended on Delaware Front a considerable distance North and South.

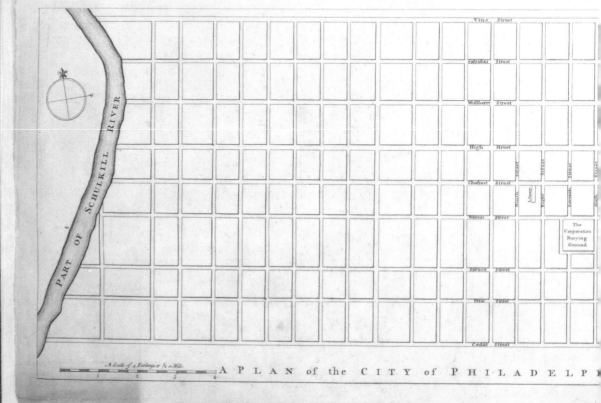

A PLAN of the CITY of PHILADELP

TUATION, HARBOUR &c. OF THE CITY AND PORT OF PHILADELPHIA.

nd, The Harbour is one of the safest & most commodious, seven or eight Fathom at low Water, & may unlade close to the Miles above tide Water, it must consequently be free from the River thirty Miles above the Town. The great distance intreated & long, and is a natural Fortification, which togetha

with a Battery a little below the Town, of twenty seven pieces of large Cannon, is thought a sufficient defence against an Attack by sea. This flourishing City was founded by the honble William Penn, first proprietor of the Province of Pennsylvania & Counties of Newcastle, Kent & Sussex on Delaware, in the Year 1682, & has increased so fast, that in the Year 1753 the number of dwelling Houses were near two thousand three hundred. The City is governed by a Mayor, Recorder, Aldermen & Common Council, is very full of Inhabitants, & their trade so extensive that there was in the Month of October last one hundred & seventeen sea Vessels in the harbour at one time, & the export from December 25. 1751, to December

25. 1752. by the Naval Office appears to be as follows. Wheat 86,530 Bushels, 125,960 Barrels of Flour 90,743 Bushels of Indian Corn, 599 Hogsheads, Tierces, 28338 Barrels, 7388 quarter Casks and 249 Tons of Bread, 925 Barrels of Beef, 5431 Barrels of Pork, 4,810,943 Staves, 1491 Bars, 189 Tons of Bar and 203 Tons of Pig Iron, 303 Chests, 32 half Chests and 15 quarter Chests of Skins & Furrs, 57 Chests, 122 Barrels & Boxes of Furrs, 5 Hogsheads of Ginseng, 9865 Hogsheads, 454 half Hogsheads, 39 Tierces and 221 Barrels of Flaxseed, & the Import from England to Philadelphia for 3 Years from Christmas 1748, to Christmas 1751, amounted to 647,267,8,9, of which 178,282,5,5, was the product & Manufacture of Gt Britain

REFERENCES.

apt Church, 6. The Court House, 7. Quakers Meeting House, 8. High Street Wharf, 9. Mulberry Street, 10. Sassafras Street, 11. Vine Street, 12. Chesnut Street, The other Streets are not to be seen from the point of Sight. 13. Drawbridge, 14. Cornhill.

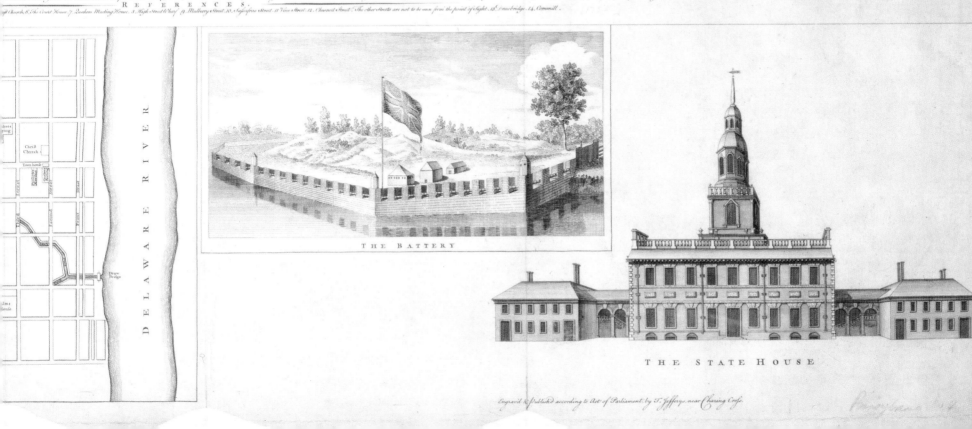

DELAWARE RIVER

Christ Church

Draw Bridge

THE BATTERY

THE STATE HOUSE

Engraved & Published according to Act of Parliament by T. Jefferys, near Charing Cross.

Georgia 1756

Right: This document was sent from North America to the British authorities on 5 January 1756 by Governor Reynolds. It shows a scheme, proposed by William Brahms, for defensive work to be undertaken at Fredericia, Savannah and Hardwick. Fort Fredericia was on St Simon's Island at the mouth of the Altamaha River, while Hardwick was at the mouth of the Ogeechee River. Savannah was founded in 1733 by General James Oglethorpe, the founding father of the state. It can lay claim to being the first town in North America that was built on a regular plan. The colony of Georgia was named after King George II, the second of the Hanoverian kings of Britain and the father of King George III. Originally established as a private enterprise, Georgia had become a crown colony in 1752, shortly before the date of this map.

Georgia 1757

Below: This map, produced by William Bonar May, is of the Creek Indian nation covering the region between the Loosa River in the west and the Chattahooche River in the east. Along with the map, the artist has also included six vignettes; on the left are a Hott house, a square and a Junker Yard, while on the right are a fort, a warrior and squaw, and Indian weapons. Founded in 1732 by James Oglethorpe, Georgia was the southernmost of the British colonies and was the last to be established. Its purpose was two-fold; first, and this was the aspect that appealed most strongly to the British government, it provided a useful buffer between the existing colonies and Spanish-controlled Florida and the land held by France. Second, it was designed as a home for people who had been imprisoned for indebtedness in Britain. Unsuccessful it reverted to Royal control in 1751.

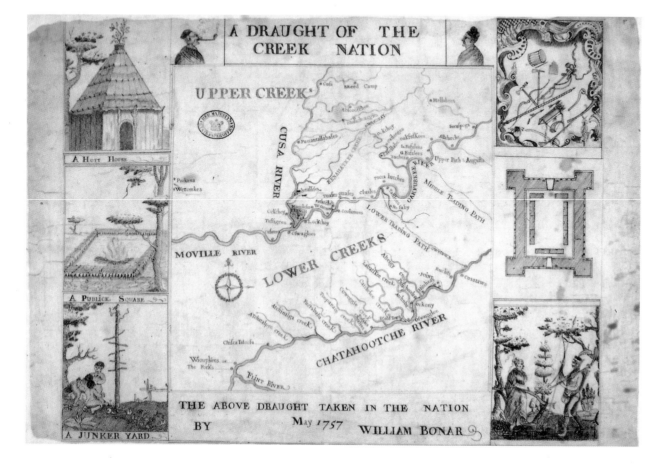

New York 1759

Right: A map of the province of New York along with part of New England (New Hampshire, Connecticut, Massachusetts and Pennsylvania) and part of New France. Compiled at a time when the French were still nominally in control of the area along the St Lawrence, this map was completed during the war which saw all French influence along the St Lawrence removed. In an era before alternative means of transport, water was the essential route by which commerce could move and it is evident here that European settlement was being concentrated along the major waterways of the region.

A MAP
OF THE PROVINCE OF
NEW YORK
PART OF
NEW ENGLAND
WITH A PART OF
NEW FRANCE
The whole Composed
from Actual Surveys
by a SCALE
16 Miles to an Inch
Done by Francis Pfister Ensign in the
1st Battalion Royal American Regt.
1759

REFERENCES.

G. Battle on the heights of Abraham gained by the British 13th September 1759.

1. Landing Place 13 Sept.r between 4 & 8 A.M.
2. British Line of Battle formed at 8 A.M.
3. Covering Detachments.

4. French Line of Battle.
5. Irregulars Posted in flying parties.

N.B. The FRENCH ARMY began the charge at 9 A.M. advancing briskly, and in good order; but a part of their line began to fire too soon, and it immediately spread throughout the whole. They then began to waver, but kept advancing with a scattered fire till they were within one hundred yards of the British, when the British Line moved up regularly, with a steady fire, and when within 20 or 30 yards of closing, gave a general fire, upon which a total route of the French ensued.

H. Works of the BRITISH ARMY on the heights of Abraham after the Victory on the 13th till the capitulation on the 18th.

6. Redoubts to cover the encampment.
7. Do. to oppose the sallies from the Town.
8. Do. to command the road to the Hospital and Bridge of the River St. Charles.
9. Do. begun but not finished before Capitulation.
10. Do. to cover the communication to the Landing Place.

a. Cape Diamond.
b. la Glaciere.
c. St. Louis.
d. St. Ursula.
e. St. John.
f. la Potasse.
g. Redoubts of Cape Diamond.
h. Royal Redoubts & Barracks.
i. Dauphiness Red.t & Barracks.
k. St. Louis.
l. St. John.
m. Palace.

List of the British Army.

15. Amhersts.
28. Braggs.
35. Otways.
43. Kennedys.
47. Lasalles. 48 Webbs.
58. Anstruthers.
78. Highlanders.
60. Royal Americans. 2 & 3 Batt.n
Light Infantry.
Artillery.
Louisburg Grenadiers.
Marines.

VIEW of QUEBEC from Point LEVI.

Plan of
QUEBEC

and ADJACENT COUNTRY Shewing

The principal ENCAMPMENTS & WORKS of the

BRITISH & FRENCH ARMIES during the SIEGE

by GENERAL WOLFE in 1759.

Reduced from the M.S.S. Map of Cap.t J.B. Clegg, by

JOHN MELISH.

REFER

A. Encampments on th
1. Landing Places
2. Magazine.
3. Hospital.

B. Encampments on
1. Church made an hospital.
2. Magazine.
3. Landing Places

C. Works at and near Poin
1. Battery of 6-32 p.rs & 5-13 in Mo
2. .. of 5-13 & 1 .10 in Sea
3. .. of 6-24 pounders.
4. .. of 8-12 pounders.

D. Encampments near the
1. Redoubts.
2. Lines.
3. Fortified Houses.

E. Works of the French alon

F. Descent of the British u
1. Landing Place.
2. Two Ketches run aground at high
Water.

of Orleans.
. Redoubts.
. Lines.
. Battery of 2 Guns.
Levi.
. Redoubts and Lines.
. Battery.
res.
. Redoubts guarded by Marines.
. Entrenched Camp.
. Cantonments to secure the Road.
. Rangers covering Road to Point Levi.
Montmorency.
. Posts for quarter guards.
. Batteries.
. Landing Place.
ts of Beauport.
orks of Beauport.
. Redoubts abandoned by the French.
. Passage of two Brigades across the
ford at low water.

Quebec 1759

Left: Produced by John Melish from an original draft by Capt J. B. Glegg, this map illustrates the siege of Quebec during the Seven Years' War (French and Indian War). Major-General James Wolfe was one of two commanders selected by the British Prime Minister, William Pitt, to lead the campaign against French possessions in North America. Prior to the siege at Quebec, British forces had captured the strategic strongpoint at Louisbourg, on the north of Cape Breton Island, on 26 July 1758; the capture of this fort meant that French supply lines to its Canadian territory were cut. The French position was further undermined by poor harvests in 1756 and 1757 and, gradually, the frontier forts fell to the advancing British. Quebec was held for the French by the Marquis de Montcalm and his position was strategically very strong. An impression of the strength of the French position can be gained by close examination of the inset, which shows a view of Quebec from the St Lawrence. On 13 September 1759, however, Wolfe launched a surprise attack when troops ascended the cliffs to the Plains of Abraham. The two armies exchanged gun fire on the Plains of Abraham, during which both Montcalm and Wolfe were fatally wounded; the latter, however, survived long enough to be told that his daring attack had proved victorious. From Quebec, British forces proceeded along the St Lawrence and captured Montreal on 8 September 1760.

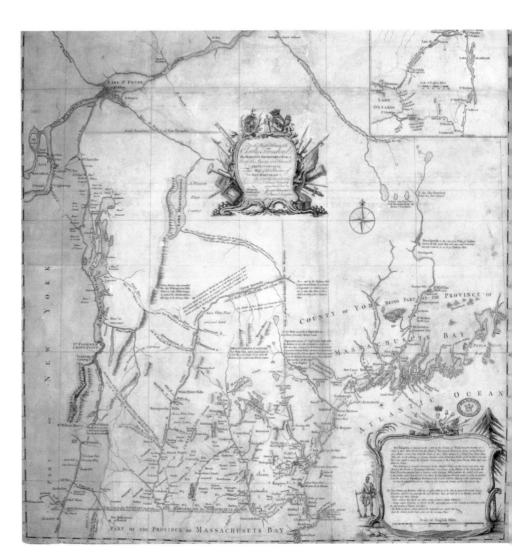

New Hampshire 1761

Above: Described as 'An accurate map of His Majesty's Province of New Hampshire in New England taken from actual surveys by Col Blanchard and the Revd Mr Langdon', this map was engraved by Thomas Jefferys and was dedicated to Charles Townshend, the Secretary of State for War, by the authors at Portsmouth, New Hampshire, on 21 October 1761. The inset map shows the St Lawrence. This map was drawn at the time of the Seven Years' War when Britain and France were contesting supremacy in North America. Charles Townshend (1725-1767) was to be a crucial figure in the history of New England; just prior to his death he introduced a number of measures as Chancellor of the Exchequer, both financial and administrative, that were known collectively as the Townshend Acts and which stimulated great opposition in the colonies.

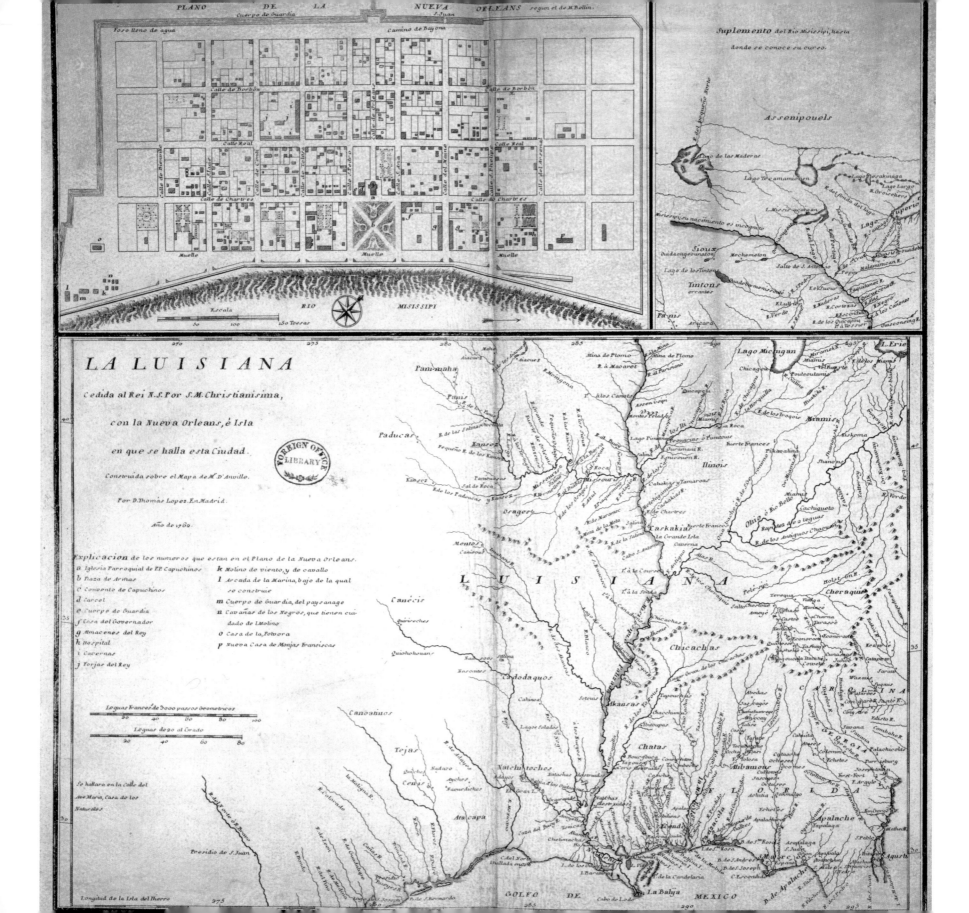

PLANO DE LA NUEVA ORLEANS segun el de M. Bellin.

Cuerpo de Guardia   S. Juan

Foso lleno de agua   Camino de Bayona

Calle de Borbón   Calle de Borbón

Calle de Orleans

Calle Real   Calle Real

Calle de Toloza   Calle de la Plaza

Calle de Chartres   Calle de Chartres

Muelle   Muelle   Muelle

RIO   MISISSIPI

Escala   50   100   150 Toesas

Suplemento del Rio Misisipi, hasta donde se conoce su curso.

Assenipouels

Lago de las Maderas

Lago Tecamamiougen

Misisipi, su nacimiento es incognito

Sioux
Ouadaougeouinaton   Mechemeton

Lago de los Tintons

Tintons errantes

Panis   Aricara

LA LUISIANA

Cedida al Rei N.S. Por S.M. Christianisima,

con la Nueva Orleans, è Isla

en que se halla esta Ciudad.

FOREIGN OFFICE LIBRARY

Construida sobre el Mapa de Mr. D'Anville.

Por D. Thomas Lopez. En Madrid.

Año de 1762.

Explicacion de los numeros que estan en el Plano de la Nueva Orleans.

a Iglesia Parroquial de P.P. Capuchinos
b Plaza de Armas
c Convento de Capuchinos
d Carcel
e Cuerpo de Guardia
f Casa del Governador
g Almacenes del Rey
h Hospital
i Cavernas
j Forjas del Rey

k Molino de viento, y de cavallo
l Arcada de la Marina, bajo de la qual se construie
m Cuerpo de Guardia, del paysanage
n Cavañas de los Negros, que tienen cuidado de LMolino
O Casa de la Polvora
p Nueva Casa de Monjas Franciscas

Se hallara en la Calle del Ave Maria, Casa de los Naturales.

Leguas Francesas de 5000 passos Geometricos
20   40   60   80   100

Leguas de 20 al Grado
20   40   60   80

LUISIANA

Pani-maha   Lago Michigan   L. Erie

Paducas   Kansez   Ilinois   Miamis

Osages   Caskakia   Ohio ó Rio Bello

Mentos   Cherakis

Canecis

Cadodaquos   Chicachas

Canoatinos   Arkansas   CAROLINA

Tejas   Chatas   GEORGIA

Natchitoches   Alibamous   FLORIDA

Cenis

Atacapa   Apalache

Presidio de S. Juan

Longitud de la Isla del Hierro

GOLFO DE MEXICO

La Balija   Cabo de Lodo   B. de Apalache

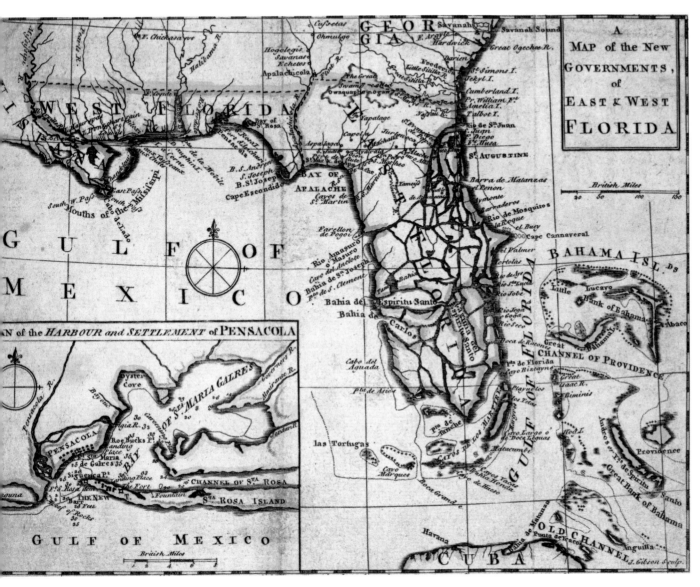

New Orleans 1762

Far left: This map of the southern part of French controlled Louisiana shows in detail the street plan of the city of New Orleans (or La Nouvelle-Orléans as it was known in French). The map is of particular note in that it was compiled by the Spanish, as the French had ceded the city to Spain in that year (although this transfer was resisted for some time by the inhabitants). The city of New Orleans was founded by the then French governor, Jean-Baptiste Lemoine de Bienville, in 1718. Its name was a tribute to the Duc d'Orléans. Three years after its foundation, New Orleans became the capital of the French colony of Louisiana. France regained the city in 1800, but it was sold to the United States as part of the Louisiana Purchase in 1803.

Florida 1765

Left: A map of the new governments of East and West Florida. This was drawn by J. Gibson and was published in the *Gentleman's Magazine*. Drawn at a scale of approximately 90 miles to one inch, the map also shows the southernmost part of Georgia and the border between West Florida and Louisiana along the Mississippi. The critical word here is 'new'; Britain had been ceded control of the former Spanish territory of Florida after the Treaty of Paris in 1763 and was to retain control until 1783 when the territory reverted to Spanish control. Pensacola, illustrated in detail as an inset, was established in 1696; it was adjacent to the best natural harbour in Florida.

Florida c1765

Right: Originally drawn by Ph. Pittman and redrawn by William Brasier, this highly detailed map — at a scale of one inch to 40ft — shows the fort of Mobile in Florida. Mobile is situated at the head of Mobile Bay at the point where the Alabama River approaches the Gulf of Mexico. It was one of a chain of forts established by the French in the late 17th and early 18th centuries along the south coast of North America. These forts guarded access to the French-controlled Mississippi. It was part of the region ceded to Britain after the Treaty of Paris in 1763.

Florida c1765

Far right: A second map originally drafted by Ph. Pittman and copied by William Brasier, shows Fort Charlotte at Mobile in relation to the surrounding country. This version of the map is drawn to a scale of 400ft to one inch.

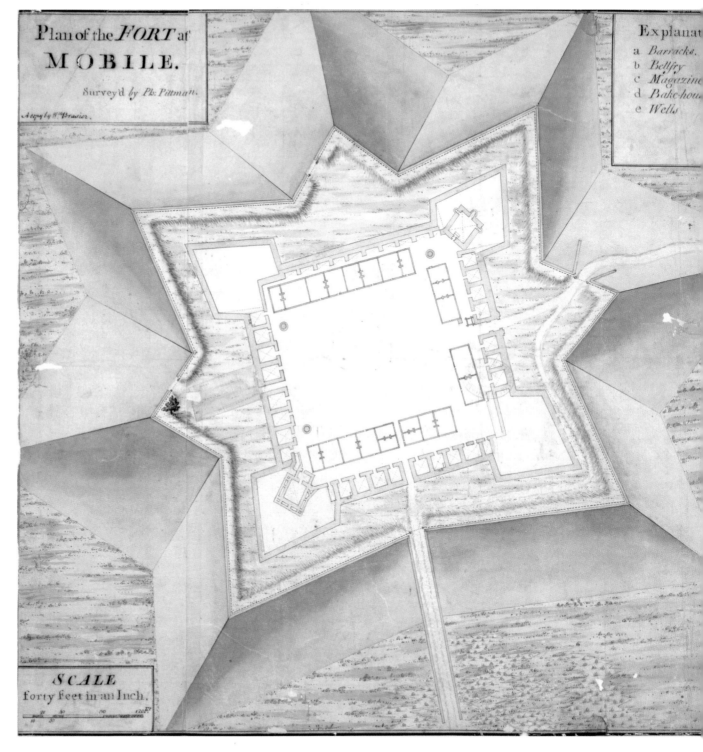

Plan of the *FORT* at MOBILE.

Survey'd *by Ph: Pittman.*

A copy by Wᵐ Brasier.

Explanat[ion]
a *Barracks.*
b *Bellfry.*
c *Magazine*
d *Bake-hou[se]*
e *Wells*

SCALE
forty feet in an Inch.

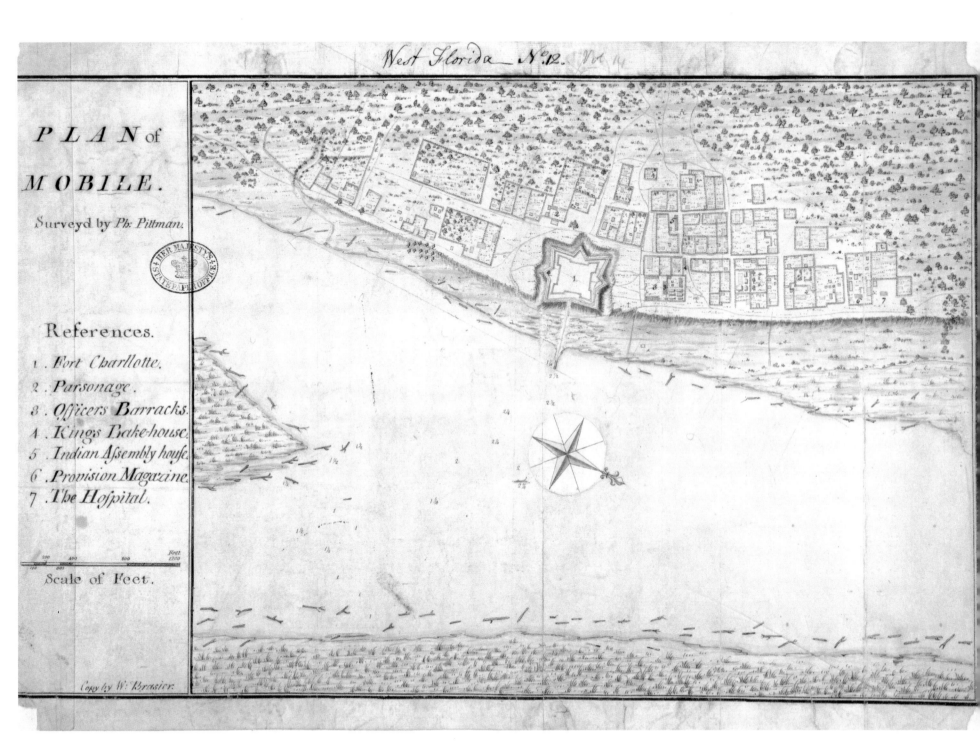

PLAN of MOBILE.

Surveyd by Ph: Pittman.

References.

1. Fort Charllotte.
2. Parsonage.
3. Officers Barracks.
4. Kings Bake-house.
5. Indian Assembly house.
6. Provision Magazine.
7. The Hospital.

Scale of Feet.

Copy by W. Brasier.

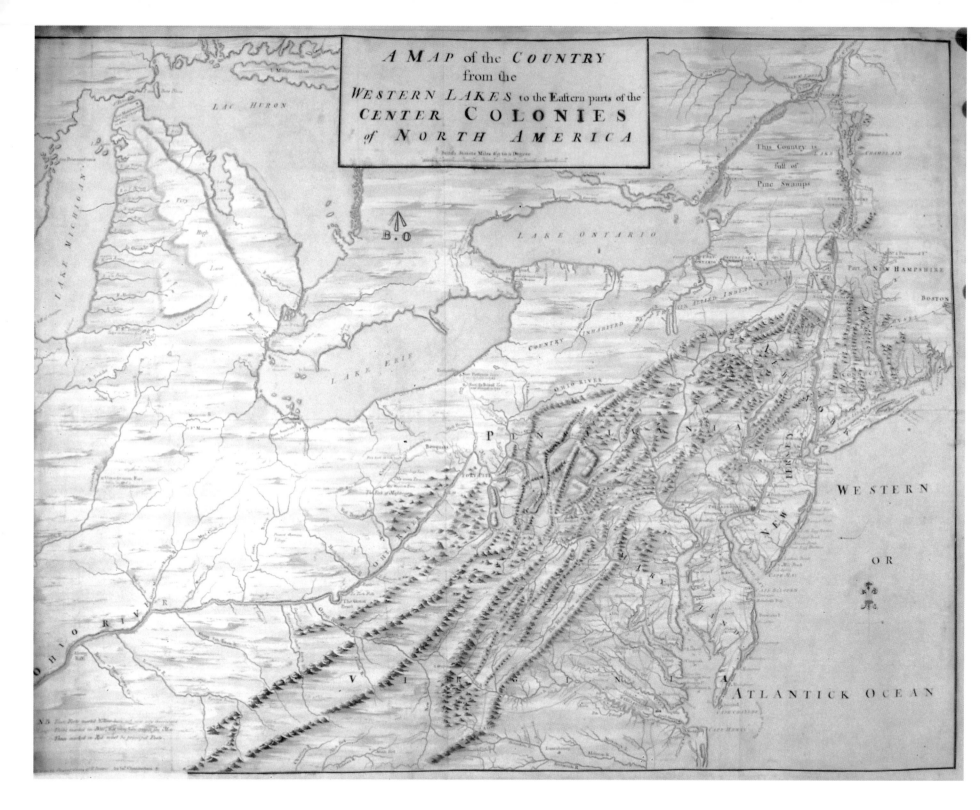

A MAP of the COUNTRY from the WESTERN LAKES to the Eastern parts of the CENTER COLONIES of NORTH AMERICA

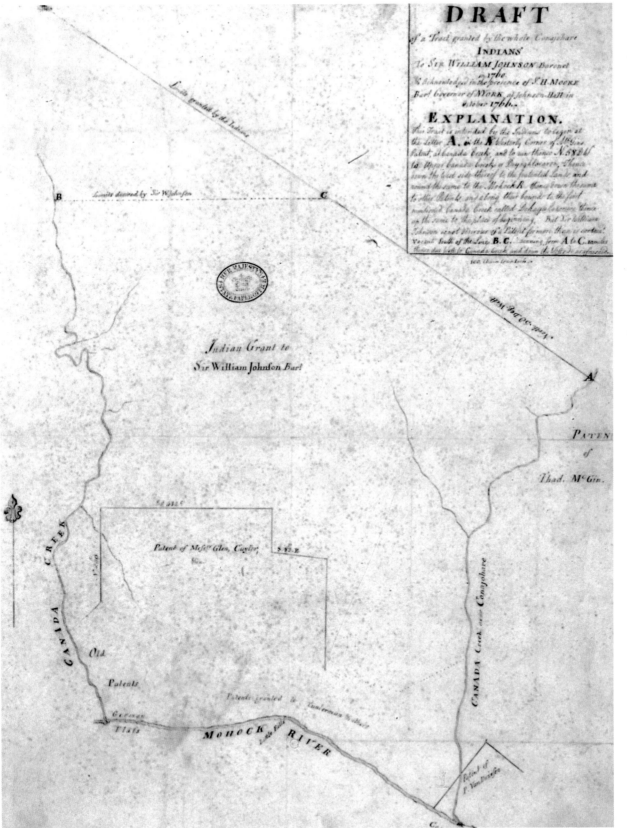

North America 1765

Far left: A map of the country from the Western Lakes to the Eastern parts of the Center Colonies of North America. The original survey for this map was undertaken by William Brasier with additional copies by John Chamberlain and Thomas Smart. The map shows the region between the original British colonies in New England and the Great Lakes, which was largely ceded to Britain by France after the Treaty of Paris in 1763. The map shows well the geographical features of the region, including the rivers and how the early settlements were, inevitably, concentrated on rivers or the coast.

New York 1766

Left: The draft of a tract granted by the whole Conajohare tribe of Indians to Sir William Johnson in 1760 and acknowledged in the presence of Sir H. Moore, Governor of New York, October 1766. Documents such as this were typical of the gradual process of European control of erstwhile Indian land, forcing the latter off their traditional lands. The area covered here is effectively the present day Herkimer County in New York state.

Lake Champlain 1767

Right: This is a copy of a map first produced in 1763 and shows, at a scale of four miles to an inch, the claims of the French and the grants made to the English reduced officers and disbanded men. Lake Champlain is situated south of the St Lawrence and forms part of the boundary between New York State and Vermont. It was named after the French explorer Samuel de Champlain, who was instrumental in exploring the St Lawrence and who founded the city of Quebec in 1608, thereby helping to establish French dominance in this part of North America. The map covers part of the territory transferred from French to British control as a result of the Treaty of Paris, 1763, after the Seven Years' War.

Quebec 1767

Far right: Design for a citadel at Quebec, 1767. This was an enclosure with a letter sent by Lt-Col Carleton on 25 November 1767 and represents a proposed defensive work for the newly captured city; in the event this was not built. The words 'Pownall 1774' were inscribed in one of the outworks at the western edge; this was perhaps in honour of Thomas Pownall, who was a colonial Governor of the period, albeit not of Quebec. The city of Quebec had been founded by the French explorer Samuel de Champlain in 1608 and had fallen to the British after General Wolfe's audacious attack upon the French settlement in 1759, which fell on 17 September of that year. This was not to be the end of the war in North America, as French forces tried to retake the city the following year. However, the Treaty of Paris in 1763 confirmed British hegemony in the region and marked the end of French power along the St Lawrence (except for the islands of St Pierre and Miquelon just to the south of Newfoundland).

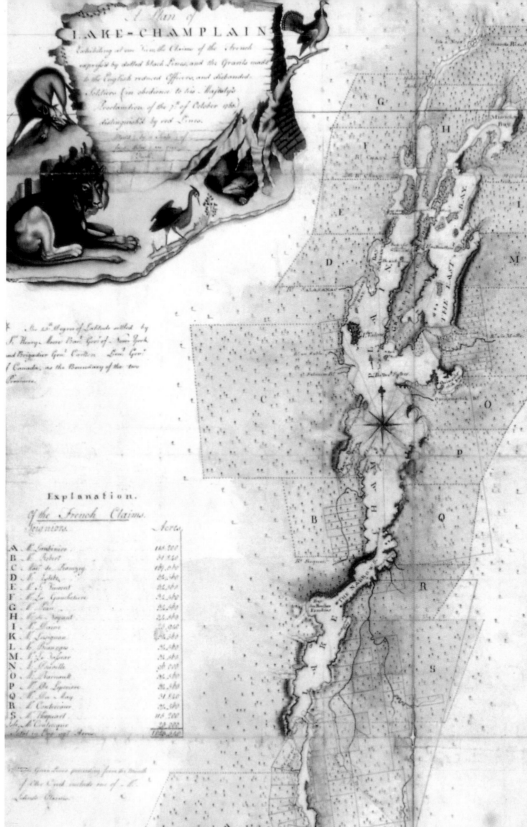

Defign for a Cittadel at Quebec 1767

North Carolina 1767

Right: As European settlement continued and their power expanded, so the buildings that were constructed became richer. This example, which demonstrates the elevation and floor plan of the governor's house to be built at New Bern in the late 1760s, shows that the neo-classical style, which was dominant in Britain at the time, also found its way to the colonies. The key describes the various rooms in the house:
A = hall; B = library; C = council room; D = dining room; E = parlour; F = housekeeper's room; G = servants' room; H = best staircase; I = lesser staircase; K = the office of the governor's secretary; L = kitchen; M = scullery; N = laundry; O = stables; P = coach house; and finally, Q = harness room.

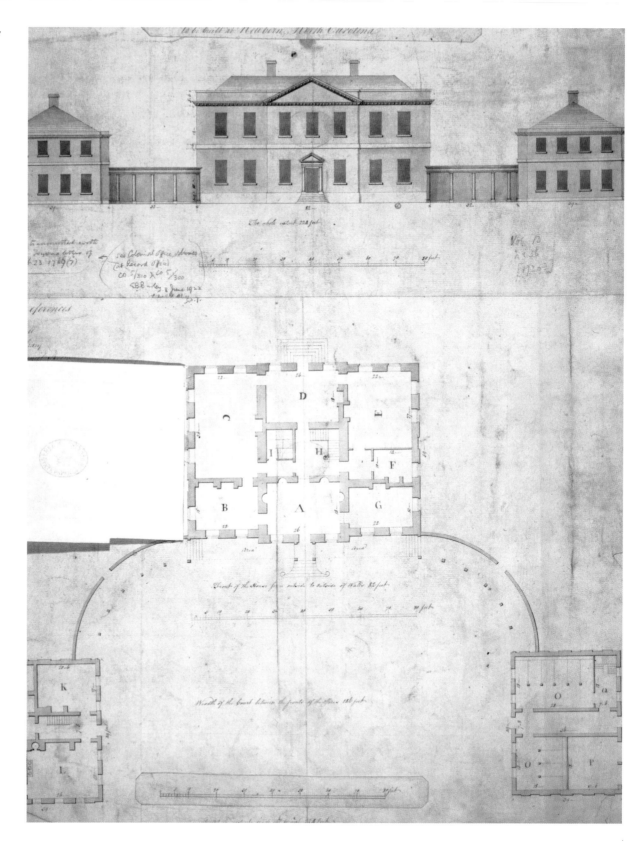

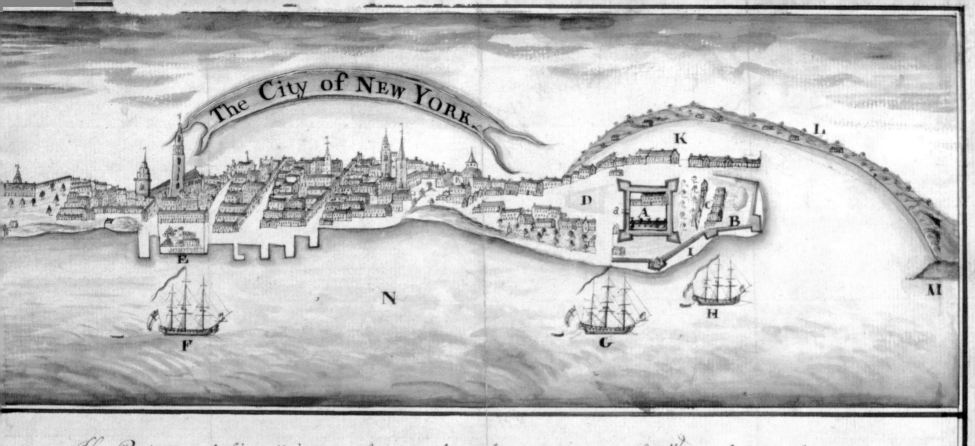

The City of NEW YORK

The Position of his Majesty's ships as they where stationed on the 1st day of November 1765:–

A. Fort George, & the Fort gate. B. The Battery. C. The Barrack. D. The Bowling green, and Broadway. E. The Kings Wharf, and Arsenal. F. His Majesty's Ship Coventry, to protect d?. G. The Guarland to scour the street and defend the Fort gate. H. The Hawke to preserve a Communication between his Majesty's Ships & the Fort, by covering the landing of boats at i. The flat Rock. K. The East River. L. Long Island. M. Governors Island. N. The North River.

W Cockburn fecit.

New York 1767

Above: This is a perspective of the city of New York across the North River showing the position of King George III's fleet as it was stationed on 1 November 1765, as well as a panorama of the city and its fort. An endorsement notes that this deployment was in connection with the riots of the Sons of Liberty following the Stamp Act Congress that met in New York in October 1765. The illustration was drawn by W. Cockburn. The Stamp Act was passed by Parliament in London, becoming law on 22 March 1765; it was an immensely unpopular act in the American colonies — 'No Taxation without Representation' — and, ultimately, was the fuse which ignited the American Revolution. The Stamp Act Congress met in New York on 7 October 1765; representatives of nine of the 13 colonies were present, and of these nine not all were official. The congress did demonstrate for the first time, however, a sense of unity of purpose amongst the colonies, although at this stage it was reform rather than revolution that was the intention. The Sons of Liberty became increasingly important in the local administration of the states, often supplanting the colonial administration, with the effect that the act was virtually unworkable. Although the Stamp Act was repealed the following year, it had fundamentally altered the relationship between Britain and its North American empire.

Part of
LAKE ERIE

le of British Miles

Ohio River

MARYLAND

VIRGINIA

PEN S **YLVANIA**

**NEW
YORK**

**NEW
JERSEY**

MAP
of the FRONTIERS of the
NORTHERN COLONIES
*with the BOUNDARY LINE established
Between them and the Indians at the Treaty
held by Sr Will. Johnson at Ft Stanwix in Novr
1768.*

Corrected and Improved from Evans Map

By Guy Johnson Dep. Agt of Ind. Affairs.

Northern Colonies 1768

Above: A map of the frontiers of the Northern Colonies with the boundary line established between them and the Indians at the Treaty held by Sir William Johnson at Fort Stanwix in November 1768. This map was originally drafted by Evans but was corrected and improved by Guy Johnson, the Deputy Agent of Indian Affairs. There were a number of treaties between the British and Indians during the years 1767 and 1771. They were designed to open up part of the old Indian reserves to the south of the Ohio River to European settlement; two new colonies were designated — Vandalia (established in 1769) and Transylvania (1775). The red line along the Ohio River is the border between these proposed new colonies and the land remaining under Indian occupation. Neither of the colonies was a success, and both failed after independence.

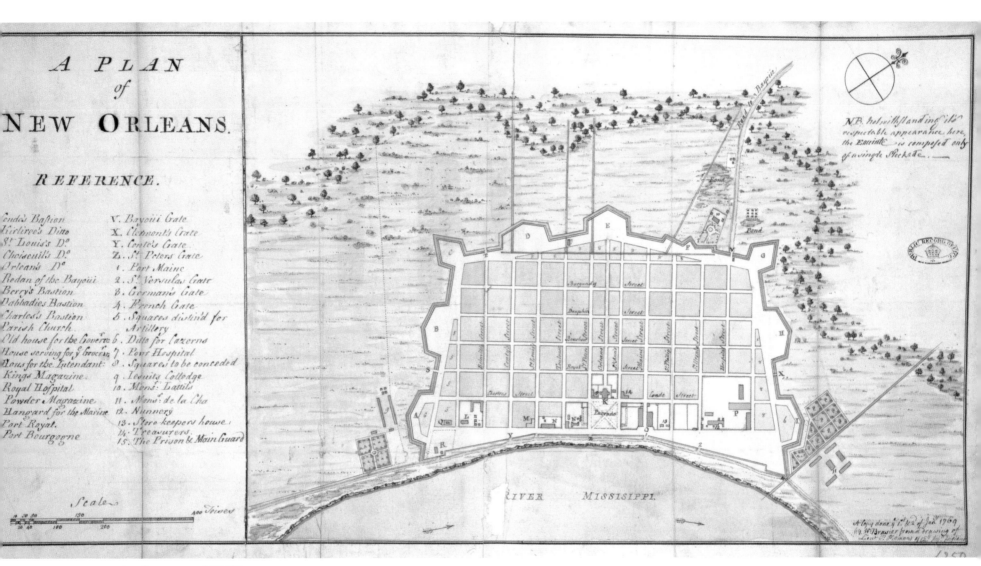

New Orleans 1769

Above: This is a copy by W. Brasier from an original drafted by Lt P. Pittman of the 15th Regiment of Engineers. The military purpose of the map, which shows in detail the disposition of the defences, is made all too clear in the annotation which reads, 'Notwithstanding its respectable appearance here, the eminente is composed only of a simple stockade'. The key gives details of the buildings and other facilities that existed in New Orleans. At this time the town was under Spanish rule, having been ceded by France — much to the opposition of the locals — earlier in the decade. The British military interest came from the proximity of the base to the recently acquired territories of West and East Florida. The French were to regain New Orleans at the end of the century and the city was acquired by the USA as part of the Louisiana Purchase of 1803. The French-Spanish involvement in the history of New Orleans remains evident to this day in the names of buildings and streets in the city.

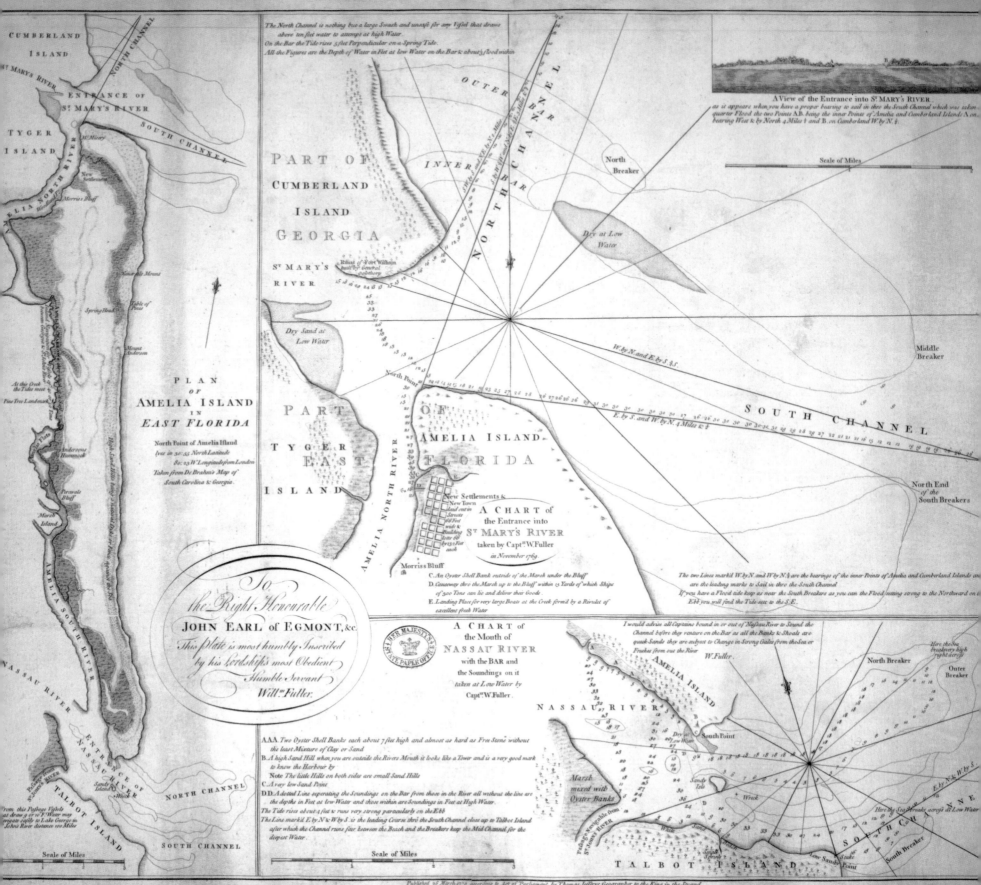

The North Channel is nothing but a large Swash and unsafe for any Vessel that draws above ten feet water to attempt at high Water
On the Bar the Tide rises 5 feet Perpendicular on a Spring Tide.
All the Figures are the Depth of Water in Feet at low Water on the Bar & about ⅓ flood within

A View of the Entrance into St MARY'S RIVER
as it appears when you have a proper bearing to sail in thro the South Channel which was taken at quarter Flood the two Points A.B. being the inner Points of Amelia and Cumberland Islands N. on bearing West & by North 4 Miles ½ and B. on Cumberland W by N. ¾.

Scale of Miles

CUMBERLAND ISLAND

St MARY'S RIVER

ENTRANCE OF St MARY'S RIVER

SOUTH CHANNEL

NORTH CHANNEL

TYGER ISLAND

PART OF CUMBERLAND ISLAND GEORGIA

St MARY'S RIVER

Ruins of Fort Within built by General Oglethorp

North Breaker

Dry at Low Water

Middle Breaker

North Point

SOUTH CHANNEL

W. by N. and E. by S. 45.

E. by S. and W. by N. 4 Miles &c

Dry Sand at Low Water

North End of the South Breakers

PLAN OF AMELIA ISLAND IN EAST FLORIDA

North Point of Amelia Island lyes in 30°.55' North Latitude 80°.23' W Longitude from London Taken from De Brahm's Map of South Carolina & Georgia.

PART OF TYGER EAST ISLAND

OF AMELIA ISLAND FLORIDA

AMELIA NORTH RIVER

New Settlements & New Town laid out in Streets 66 Feet wide & Building lots 60 by 132 Feet each

A CHART of the Entrance into St MARY'S RIVER taken by Captn W. Fuller in November 1769

Morriss Bluff

C. An Oyster Shell Bank outside of the Marsh under the Bluff
D. Causeway thro the Marsh up to the Bluff within 15 Yards of which Ships of 300 Tons can lie and deliver their Goods
E. Landing Place for very large Boats at the Creek form'd by a Rivulet of excellent fresh Water

The two Lines mark'd W. by N. and W by N.¾ are the bearings of the inner Points of Amelia and Cumberland Islands and are the leading marks to Sail in thro the South Channel
If you have a Flood tide keep as near the South Breakers as you can the Flood setting strong to the Northward on the Ebb you will find the Tide sett to the S.E.

To the Right Honourable JOHN EARL of EGMONT, &c.
This plate is most humbly Inscribed by his Lordship's most Obedient Humble Servant Willm Fuller.

A CHART of the Mouth of NASSAU RIVER with the BAR and the Soundings on it taken at Low Water by Captn W. Fuller

HER MAJESTY'S STATE PAPER OFFICE

I would advise all Captains bound in or out of Nassau River to Sound the Channel before they venture on the Bar as all the Banks & Shoals are quick Sands they are subject to Change in Strong Gales from the Sea or Freshes from out the River
W. Fuller.

NASSAU RIVER

ENTRANCE OF NASSAU RIVER

AMELIA ISLAND

AMELIA BAR

North Breaker

Outer Breaker

Here the Sea breakers high right across

NASSAU RIVER

South Point

Dry at Low Water

Sandy Isle

Wreck

AAA. Two Oyster Shell Banks each about 7 feet high and almost as hard as Free Stone without the least Mixture of Clay or Sand
B. A high Sand Hill when you are outside the Rivers Mouth it looks like a Tower and is a very good mark to know the Harbour by
Note The little Hills on both sides are small Sand Hills
C. A very low Sand Point
DD. A dotted Line separating the Soundings on the Bar from those in the River all without the line are the depths in Feet at low Water and those within are Soundings in Feet at High Water.
The Tide rises about 4 feet & runs very strong particularly on the Ebb
The Line mark'd E by N & W by S. is the leading Course thro the South Channel close up to Talbot Island after which the Channel runs fair between the Beach and the Breakers keep the Mid Channel for the deepest Water.

Marsh mixed with Oyster Banks

Leading mark seen from St Marys RIVER

TALBOT ISLAND

White Sand

SOUTH CHANNEL

South Breaker

Here the Sea breaks across at Low Water

E. by N & W by S.

Low Sandy Point

NORTH CHANNEL

SOUTH CHANNEL

NASSAU RIVER

TALBOT ISLAND

Sandy Island

AMELIA SOUTH RIVER

Scale of Miles

Scale of Miles

Published 28 March 1770 according to Act of Parliament by Thomas Jefferys Geographer to the King in the Strand.

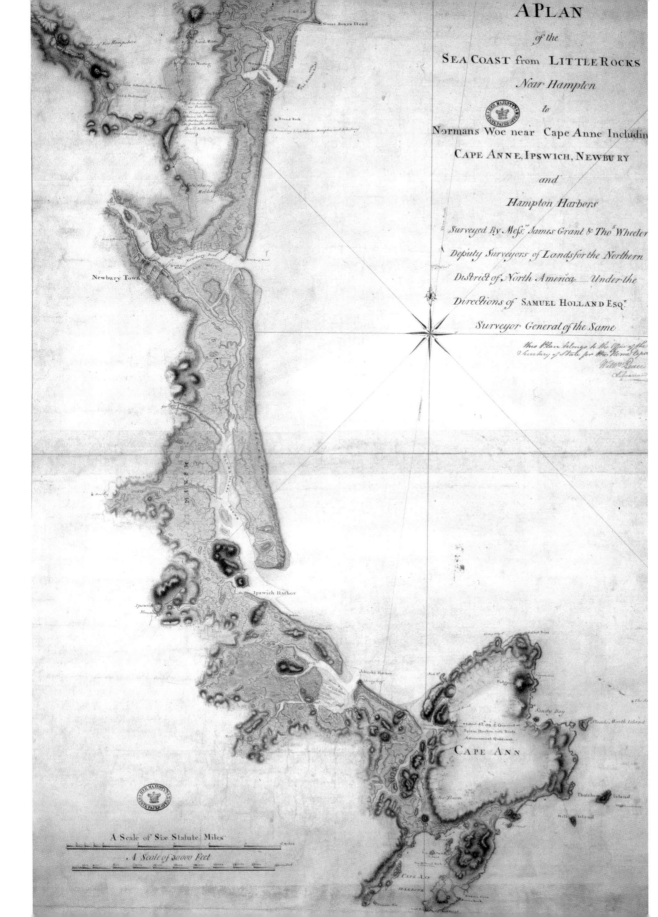

A PLAN

of the

SEA COAST from LITTLE ROCKS

Near Hampton

to

Normans Woe near Cape Anne Includin

CAPE ANNE, IPSWICH, NEWBURY

and

Hampton Harbors

Surveyed By Mess.rs James Grant & Thos Wheeler

Deputy Surveyors of Lands for the Northern

District of North America Under the

Directions of SAMUEL HOLLAND ESQ.r

Surveyor General of the Same

A Scale of Six Statute Miles

A Scale of 30000 Feet

Florida 1770

Far left: This map of Florida was published in London on 26 March 1770 by Thomas Jefferys and was drawn originally by William Fuller. The map is dedicated to John Earl of Egmont. The maps were designed for maritime purposes and Fuller includes advice for mariners; this advice includes the comment: 'I would advise all captains bound in or out of Nassau River to sound the channel before they venture on the bar as all the banks and shoals are quick sands they are subject to change in strong gales from the sea or freshes from out the river.' The new town marked is the position today occupied by Fernandina Beach. Florida had been a Spanish territory, but passed to British control after the Treaty of Paris in 1763; following the Revolutionary War Florida reverted to Spanish rule in 1783.

Massachusetts 1770

Left: This is a plan of the sea coast of Massachusetts from Little Rocks, near Hampton, to Normans Woe, near Cape Anne. Also included is information about the harbours at Hampton, Cape Anne, Ipswich and Newbury (now Newburyport). It was surveyed by James Grant and Thomas Wheeler, Deputy Surveyors of Lands for the Northern District of North America, under the direction of Samuel Holland, Surveyor General. This is the section of the Massachusetts coast to the south of New Hampshire. The border between New Hampshire and Massachusetts is to the north of the river at Newbury. On Cape Anne can be seen 'Gloster Town'; this is the modern day Gloucester. In 1775 New Hampshire was the first colony to depose its British governor, thereby leading the way towards independence.

Florida 1771

Above: This is a map of Beauclerk's Bluff Plantation on the east side of the
river of St John's in the province of East Florida. It was drawn, the legend reads,
from an actual survey carried out in 1771 by Joseph Purcell. In addition to
showing the plantation, the map also shows place names, roads, direction of
currents and other information. The scale is about seven chains to one inch. East
and West Florida — the two representing the modern state — had originally
been a Spanish colony. The Floridas were, however, regarded by the Spaniards
more for their strategic location defending the sea lanes from central America
rather than as a source of colonial development. The colony was seized by the
British during the War of 1756-1763, a seizure that was confirmed by the Treaty
of Paris in 1763. The results of this war were dramatic; the British empire in
North America had grown enormously, but at some cost. The National Debt had
increased and the new Empire had to be paid for; these factors were at the heart
of the issue which led to the 'No Taxation without Representation' claims and
ultimately to the Revolutionary War. Florida reverted to Spanish rule in 1783 after
the second Treaty of Paris — which settled the Revolutionary War — finally
becoming part of the United States in 1819.

Alabama/Florida 1772

Right: A plan of part of the rivers Tombecbe [Tombigbee], Alabama, Tensa
[Tensaw], Perdito and Scambia [Conecut] in the province of West Florida 'with a
sketch of the boundary between the nation of the Upper Creek Indians and that
part of the province which is contiguous thereto as settled at the Congresses at
Pensacola in the years 1765 and 1771.' The map was drawn by David Taitt on the
orders of John Stuart, Superintendent of Indian Affairs. The map gives both the
Indian and English names of rivers. West Florida was ceded by Spain to Britain at
the Treaty of Paris in 1763; the area to the north was designated as an Indian
reserve, although it was in the British sphere of influence. The area which is
today known as Alabama, situated to the north of Florida, was ceded by France to
Britain after 1763 and in 1783, following the British defeat in the Revolutionary
War, the southern section passed to Spain (along with Florida). Alabama became
a US territory in 1817 and became the 22nd state in 1819.

North and South Carolina 1772

Above: This is 'An exact map of the boundary line between the provinces of North and South Carolina agreeable to the royal instruction — certified by the commissioners and surveyors of the two provinces on 4 June 1772'. The map is signed by the various dignitaries involved. The surveyors for North Carolina were Thomas Rutherford and Thomas Polk. The surveyors for South Carolina were James Cook and Ephraim Mitchell. The North's commissioners were John Rutherford and William Dry whilst those for the South were William Moultrie and William Thompson. The accompanying note from Governor Martin described the plan as 'an original draft made upon the spot' and apologised for its roughness. Maps like this were of fundamental importance in establishing the ownership of specific territory; although it is easy to see the 'Thirteen Colonies' as a complete entity, at this time there was no central power and each colony or province regarded its territorial integrity as paramount. It is interesting to note that, although the colonies were given separate administrations in 1729, it was only at this stage, in the period immediately before the British lost control, that detailed boundaries were drawn up.

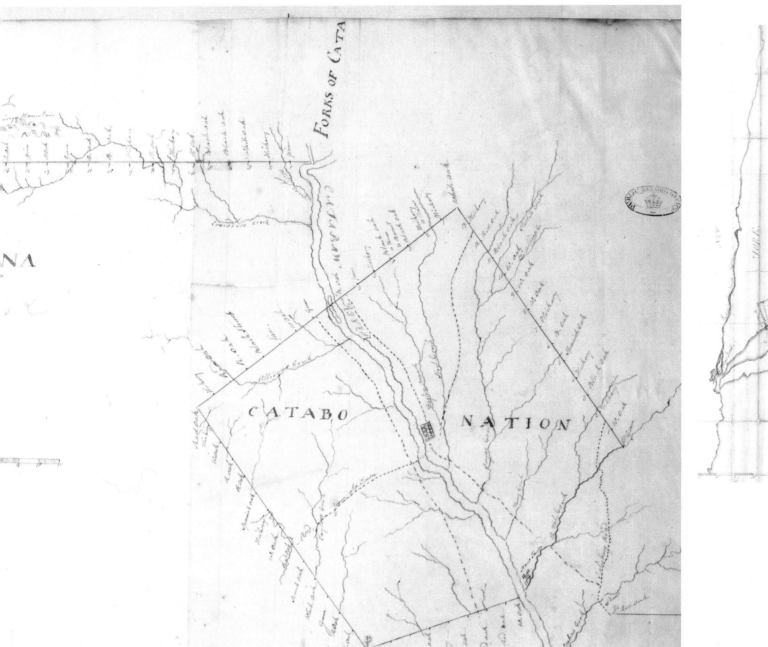

Connecticut 1774

Above right: Drawn by J. Trumbull in 1774, this map shows Connecticut from Cape Cod to Fort Pitt. The first explorer of the Connecticut River was a Dutchman, Adrian Block, in 1614, but it was the English Puritans who were at the forefront of the European settlement of the region. In 1634 Windsor was established as the first European settlement and the future state was founded the following year by Thomas Hooker. Connecticut was one of four colonies that were to be founded from settlers already established in Massachusetts. Initially, the settlers faced threats from the local Pequot Indians. The Pequot War of 1636-37 was one of a number of campaigns waged by the early settlers against the indigenous population. English anger had been caused by the Pequot trading exclusively with the Dutch and, following the murder of a Boston trader, a force of 120 settlers and sympathetic Indians attacked the Pequot. Some 500 Pequot were massacred on the Mystic River, whilst others were killed on the Connecticut and Housatonic rivers. The colony received its Royal Charter in 1662, the same year as when Connecticut incorporated the smaller colony of New Haven. New Haven became the home of Yale University, founded in 1716.

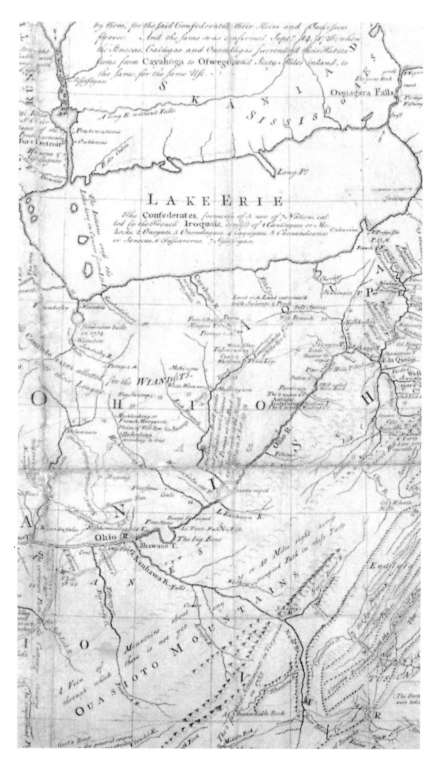

North America 1775

Left (detail) and Below: Compiled just before the Revolutionary War that was to see North America divided between British-ruled Canada and the independent United States of America, this map was a copy of an earlier map (dating from 1755 and compiled by Lewis Evans) which shows British power in the region at its peak. The legend reads that the original 1755 map had been 'since corrected and improved, as also extended with the addition of New England and bordering parts of Canada; from actual surveys now lying at the Board of Trade [in London]. By T. Pownall. Printed and published for J. Almon, Piccadilly, London 25 March 1776'. It is a sobering thought that, while this map was being prepared for printing in London, thousands of miles away, in the regions depicted, events were occurring that would shape the future destiny of the world; it was in the autumn of 1775 that the first moves to change the constitution started to gather momentum and in the spring of 1776 this process was accelerated. It was on 2 July 1776 that Congress approved the resolutions that marked the formal declaration of independence; approval that was ratified by vote on 4 July.

Pennsylvania 1775

Right: This map of Pennsylvania exhibits not just the improved parts of the province but also its extensive frontiers laid down from actual surveys — chiefly from the map of W. Scull published in 1770 — and 'humbly inscribed to the Honourable Thomas Penn and Richard Penn, true and absolute proprietors and governors of the province of Pennsylvania'. It was published in London on 10 June 1775 and was drawn to a scale of six miles to one inch. Pennsylvania had been founded by William Penn in the 17th century as a colony for Quakers; it had been named by King Charles II after Admiral Penn, the founder's father. Although established for Quakers, the colony's religious toleration, along with its natural resources, made it a sensible destination for many of those coming from Europe during the 18th century. As a result a disparate population, including many Germans and Dutch, became established. The charter granting William Penn the right to create the colony ensured that this inheritance was passed down through his family. It was only following the Declaration of Independence — the year after this map was published — and the Revolutionary War that the proprietorial rights held by families like the Penns were ended. The southernmost part of the map includes part of Maryland; the border between Pennsylvania and Maryland is the famous Mason-Dixon line.

Boston 1776

Left (detail) and Below: This is a plan of Boston, Massachusetts, and its environs showing in detail the military works undertaken in 1775 and 1776. The map is dedicated to Lord George Germain, Secretary of State, by the author/publisher Henry Pelham. It was engraved in aquatint by Francis Jukes and published in London on 2 June 1777. Settled by the British in 1630 and named after the home town of their leader — Boston in Lincolnshire — Boston was one of the centres of British colonialism in the 'Thirteen Colonies' and was also to be a centre of the revolution that led to independence. On 5 March 1770 the Boston Massacre occurred, when British soldiers fired upon unarmed civilians. Although the actual details are uncertain, it would appear that a group of youths pelted an army patrol with snowball and stones outside the customs house; feeling threatened, the troops fired, ultimately killing five. Three years later, and in response to another piece of hated legislation from London (the Tea Act), Bostonians raided the harbour on 16 December 1773 and threw 340 chests of tea into the water. The date of this map is significant because it shows the defences that the British authorities erected as a counter measure to the increasing threats to their colonial power. Once war broke out, Boston was held by the British until 4 March 1776, when American troops led by Washington crossed the Charles River, captured the Dorchester Heights and forced the British to retreat.

Canada 1777

Right (detail) and inset: A map of the inhabited part of Canada from French surveys; with the frontiers of New York and New England from a large survey by Claude Joseph Sauthier. The map was engraved and published by William Faden at Charing Cross in London in early 1777. The map is dedicated to Major-General John Burgoyne and the location of the winter quarters of the British forces under his command in 1776 are given. Apart from the location of the British forces, note also the border along the 45th parallel between Canada and New York along with the earlier proposals and the importance of the St Lawrence as the main route for travel and transport. The population of Canada was concentrated along the river and on the coast of the Great Lakes until the coming of railways in the mid-19th century. General Burgoyne was one of the main British commanders during the Revolutionary War. He had an army of some 7,000 men in Canada and planned to march south splitting the rebel forces in half. This plan failed dismally and he was forced to surrender to General Horatio Gates at Saratoga on 17 October 1777.

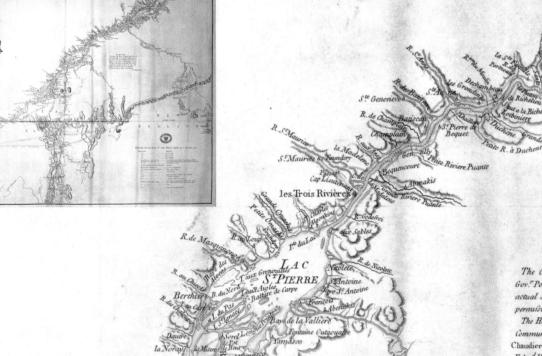

REMARKS.

The Course of the River St. Francis is laid down in Govr. Pownalls Map of the Mid. Brit. Colonies from an actual Survey made by Major Holland and by the Govr. permission is here Copied. Vide Topogl. Descn. pa. 14 & 15.

The Head of Kennebec from Norridge Walk and the Communications between that River & the Sources of the Chaudiere were Survey'd by Order of Govr. Pownall by Edwd. Howard under the direction of Captn. Nicholls.

Vide Topogl. Descn. pa. 22.

Chateau Richer
Longue Pointe
I. D'ORLEANS
Lorette Huron Charlebourg
QUEBEC
Beaumont
Rivière Boyer

R. St. Anne
Ste. Genevieve
R. de Champlain
Batiscan
Champlain
S. Maurice & Foundery
Pointe du Lac
les Trois Rivières
Cap Lieutenant

R. St. Maurice
la Madelen
Bequencourt
Abenakis
Grande Rivière Puante
Petite Rivière Puante
aux Sables

River St. François

R. de Nicolete
Nicolete
St. Antoine
Baye St. Antoine
François
Abenakis

R. de Masquinonge
LAC St. PIERRE
Baye de la Vallière
Fontaine Outacuatie
Yamaska

R. au Chicot
Baye des Vovees
aux Grenouilles
Berthier
B. du Nord
aux Aiglas
Battière de Carpe
L. du Pas
L. St. Ignace
Dautre
Sorel Longueüil
Yamaska R.
la Neray
de Misere
B. d. Baye
B. d. Yamaska
la Valérie
S. Ours
I. Chaillon
I. Dervy

R. de L'Assomption
S. Sulpice
Contrecœur
Moushard
St. Antoine
L'Assomption
Verchères
St. Charles
L. Bourd
Riv. de Richelieu
la Chenaye
S. Michel

Terrebonne & Jean
Varenne
Commune
Boucherville
Utawas River
les deux Montagnes
Canasadoga Iroquois
Isle Jesus
Rose
Trembley
Longueil
Ste. Helene
Montagne Bizare
MONTREAL
St. Laurent
St. Lambert
Richelieu
Belæil
Lac des deux Montagnes
Kinchin
S. Paul
St. Joseph
St. Louis
Brussy
la Prairie de la Madelne
Bassin de Chambly
Pointe Olivier
Bout of Chambly
Rapide Perret
I. Perrot
Lac St. Louis
Fort Chambly
Portage
L. St. Therese
Bridelour
Chateauguai Iroquois
Cachenouaga Iroquois
Cotau des Cédres
Rapide du Côteau des Cedres
Savne.
Rapid St. John
Pt. R. du Nord
Fort Ste. John

Pte. au Foin
River Chateaugai
River aux Cutardes
Montreal R.
R. Saenpa en R. de la Torue
Pt. R. du Nord
Pt. R. du Sud
Chambly R.
Narrows
6 Feet Bar

LAC St. FRANCOIS
West Branch of R. Chateaugai
East Branch
R. Bleury
L. aux Noix
Gd. R. du Sud

C   **A**   **N**   **A**   **D**   **A**

Rapide
Falls
Fall
Fall
Rapid

MEMBRAHABEGEK
Dien still Water
Rocky R.

Height of the Land the Boundary between Canada and New E.
Heads of Connecticut River
Great and Little Monadnick Mountains

Colonel Arnold's Rout in
River Chaudiere chiefly Inhabited on both side

Carleton

LAKE

Prattsburgh
East Bay
Dean B.
St. François
Whitewood I.
Missiskoui R.
Salmon Fishery
Beekman
proposed Boundary
Bois blancs
Saladam

NEW   **Y**   **O**   **R**   **K**   **E**   **N**

Puerto Rico 1780

Right: This map shows Puerto Rico with towns, churches and forts delineated by pictograms. The name 'Puerto Rico' means 'Rich Harbour' in Spanish and, with gold as a source of wealth, the island was quickly developed after its discovery by Columbus in 1493. The first permanent settlement was led by Juan Ponce de Leon in 1508. The island was to remain Spanish until 1898 when, following a short US-Spanish war, it was ceded to the USA. Puerto Ricans were granted US citizenship in 1917, but in November 1993 they voted to maintain the island's status and against incorporation into the United States.

Savannah 1799

Below: Plan of the siege by French and American forces of Savannah, Georgia, and of the attack of 9 October 1779. Savannah lies on the Atlantic coast of Georgia at the estuary of the Savannah River which forms the boundary between South Carolina and Georgia. It was founded in 1733 by Gen. James E. Oglethorpe, the founder of the colony of Georgia. The French alliance was crucial to the ultimate success of the revolutionaries in the Thirteen Colonies. On 6 February 1778 the French signed two treaties with the Americans — a treaty of amity and commerce, and one of alliance. This guaranteed French military support for the rebels and changed fundamentally British strategy, forcing them to divert vitally important military equipment to the defence of Britain from French attack. The siege and capture of Savannah was to be one of the first successes of the American-French alliance. It was a serious blow to the British, who had believed that both Georgia and South Carolina would remain loyal. In fact, the final campaign of the War of Independence was to be fought in the Carolinas and Virginia, resulting in the ultimate capitulation of Gen. Cornwallis and the British army at Yorktown on 19 October 1781.

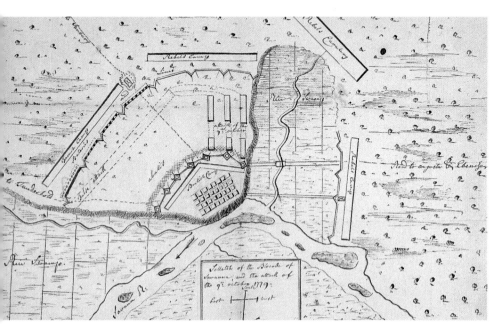

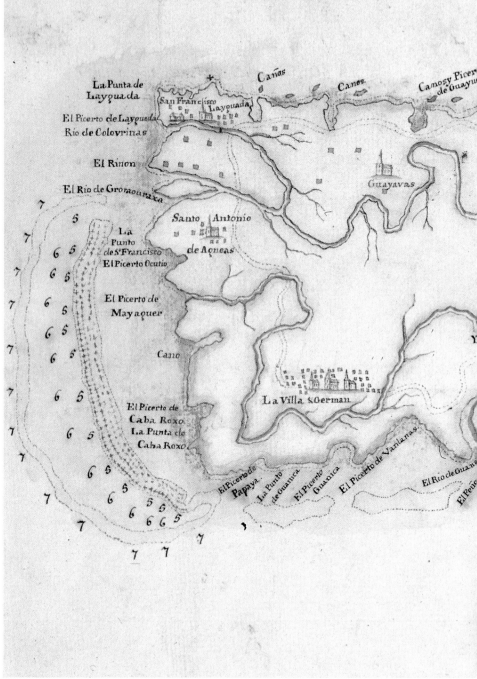

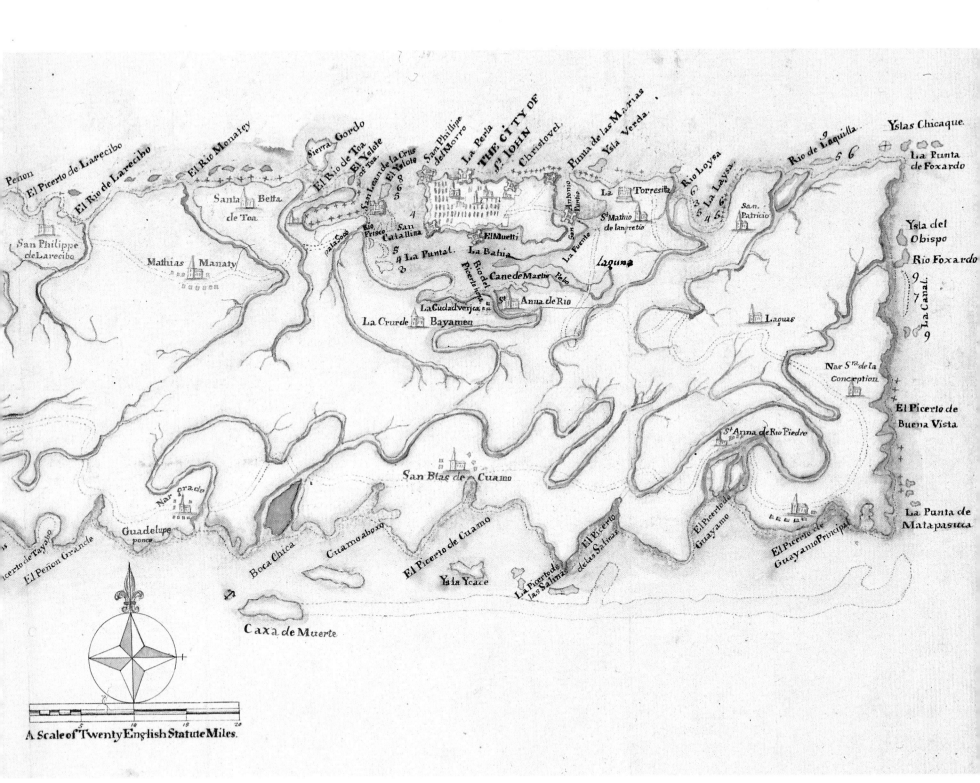

Penon
El Picerto de Larecibo
El Rio de Larecibo
El Rio Monatey
Sierra Gordo
El Rio de Toa
El Yslote
of Toa
San Leon de la Crus
El Yslote
La Perla
San Phillipe del Morro
THE CITY OF
S.t IOHN
Christovel
Punta de las Marias
Ysla Verda
Rio Loysa
Rio de Laquilla
Yslas Chicaque.
San Philippe de Larecibo
Santa Betta
de Toa
La Laysa
La Punta
de Foxardo
La Torresilla
San
Patricio
Ysla del
Obispo
Rio Foxardo
Mathias   Manaty
Rio,
Frisco
San
Catallina
San Antonio
Fuente
S.t Mathio
de langretio
La Fuente
La Canal.
El Muelti
La Puntal.
La Bahia
Laguna
La Crur de   Bayamen
La Cudad verja
S.t Anna de Rio
Cane de Marbu
Rio del
Picerto Hotu
Palo
Laguas
Nar S.ra de la
Conception
St Anna de Rio Piedre
El Picerto de
Buena Vista
San Blas de   Cuamo
Nar orade
El Picerto de
Guayamo
La Punta de
Matapasuca
Guadelupe
ponce
Boca Chica
Cuamo aboxo
El Picerto de Cuamo
Ysla Ycace
La Picerto de
las Salinas
El Picerto
de las Salinas
El Picerto de
Guayamo Principal
El Penon Grande
icerto de Tayao
Caxa de Muerte

A Scale of Twenty English Statute Miles.

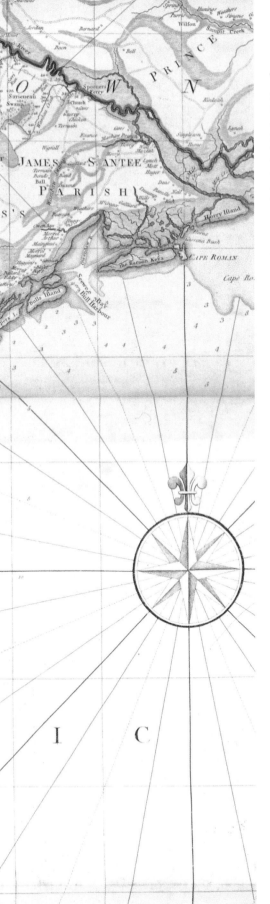

South Carolina 1780

Left (detail) and Right: A map of South Carolina and part of Georgia containing the whole seacoast, islands, inlets, rivers, creeks, parishes, townships, boroughs, roads and bridges. Published by William Faden in London in 1780 from surveys undertaken by the Honourable William Bull, Lieutenant Governor, Captain Hugh Bryan and William de Brahm, Surveyor General of the Southern District of North America. The map also includes a table referring to the ownership of land in South Carolina. English settlement of North and South Carolina started in 1663 when Charles II gave a charter to eight proprietors for the development of the new colony. The Carolinas were divided into two in 1689. At the centre of the map, at the end of a peninsula where the Ashley River meets the Cooper River, is Charles Town (Charleston), founded in 1670. The Ashley and Cooper rivers gained their names from Anthony Ashley Cooper, later Earl of Shaftesbury, who was one of the most influential figures in the establishment of the Carolina colonies.

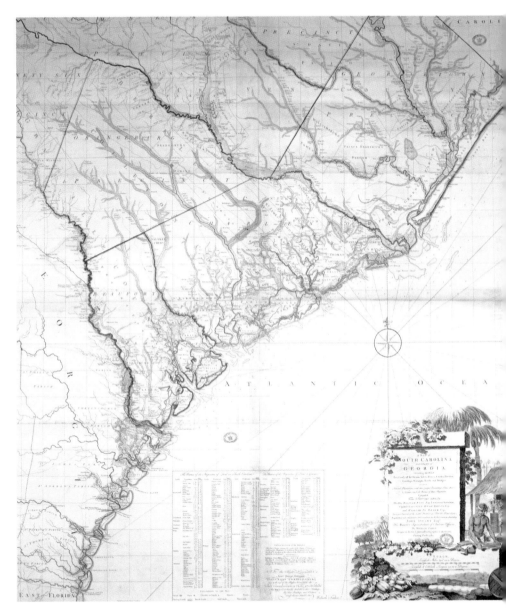

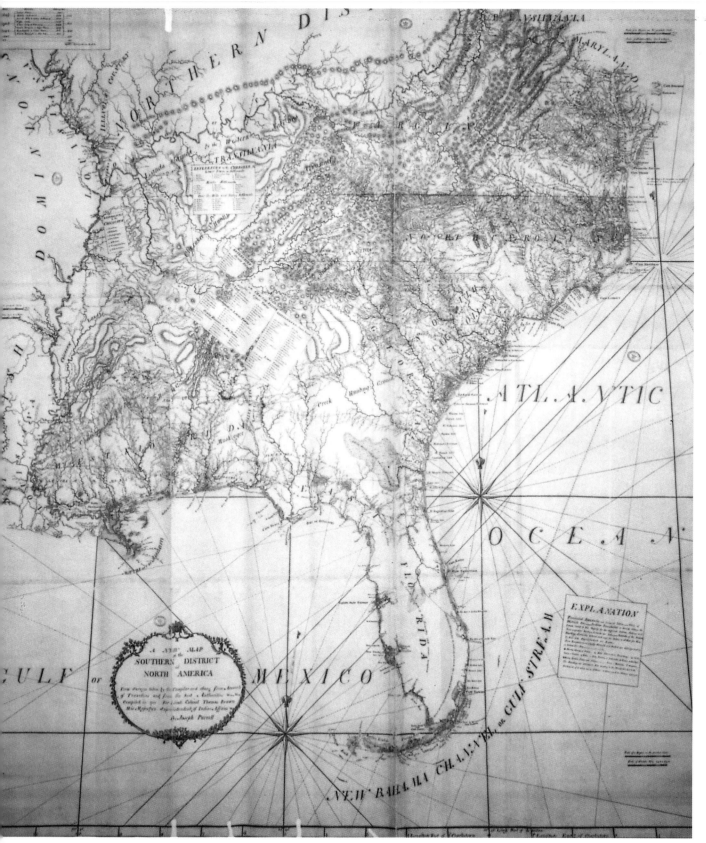

Southern Colonies 1781

Left: Produced at the height of the Revolutionary War, this is described as 'A new map of the Southern District of North America. From surveys taken by the compiler and others . . . compiled in 1781. For Lieutenant-Colonel Thomas Brown, Superintendent of India Affairs by Joseph Purcell'. The scale is about 16 miles to one inch with longitude measured from Charleston. There is a table of explanation of boundaries of provincial and Indian lands. There is also a table giving the numbers of Indian fighting men. The map includes East and West Florida; at this time Florida was part of the British-ruled area of North America. However, with the Treaty of Paris that confirmed United States independence in 1783, Florida was returned to Spanish rule.

Kentucky 1784

Right: 'This map of Kentucke (sic), drawn from actual observations is inscribed with the most perfect respect to the honourable the Congress of the United States of America and to his excellency George Washington, later Commander in Chief of their army by their humble servant John Filson'. Drawn to a scale of 10 miles to an inch and with a key illustrating stations or forts, salt springs, dwelling houses and mills, and wigwams, the map shows Kentucky immediately after independence. It was engraved by Henry D. Pursell and printed by T. Rook. The area which was to form Kentucky was settled by both the British and the French. It was to become the 15th state of the Union on 1 June 1792.

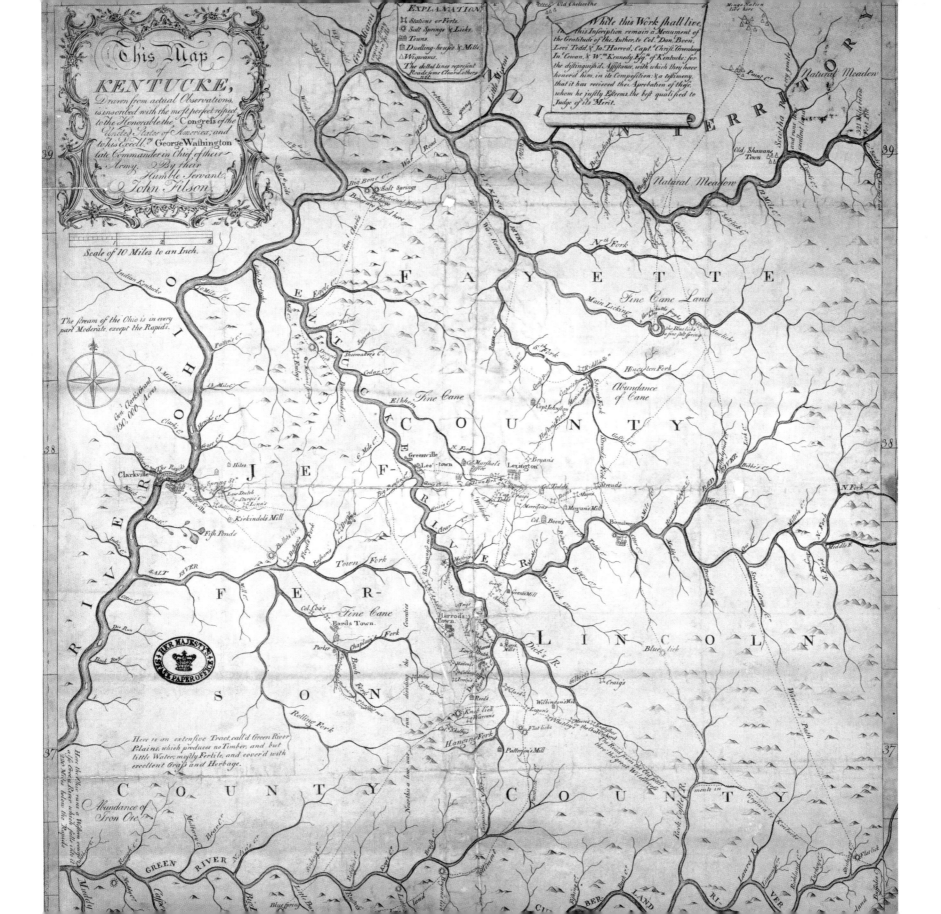

This Map of KENTUCKE, Drawn from actual Observations, is inscribed with the most perfect respect, to the Honorable the Congress of the United States of America; and to his Excell.y George Washington late Commander in Chief of their Army. By their Humble Servant, John Filson

Scale of 10 Miles to an Inch.

EXPLANATION.
Stations or Forts.
Salt Springs & Licks.
Towns.
Dwelling-houses & Mills.
Wigwams.
The dotted lines represent Roads some Clear'd others not.

While this Work shall live, let this Inscription remain a Monument of the Gratitude of the Author, to Col. Dan. Boon, Levi Todd, & Ja. Harrod, Capt. Christ. Greenbury In.o Cowan, & W.m Kennedy Esq.r of Kentucke: for the distinguish'd Assistance, with which they have honored him, in its Composition; & a testimony, that it has received the Aprobation of those, whom he justly Esteems, the best qualified to Judge of its Merit.

The stream of the Ohio is in every part Moderate, except the Rapids.

Gen.l Clarks tract 150,000 Acres

Here is an extensive Tract, call'd Green River Plains, which produces no Timber, and but little Water, mostly Fertile, and cover'd with excellent Grass and Herbage.

Abundance of Iron Ore.

INDIAN TERRITORY

Natural Meadow
Old Shawana Town
Natural Meadow

FAYETTE
Fine Cane Land
Fine Cane
Abundance of Cane

COUNTY

O H I O   R I V E R

JEFF-ERSON

FER-SON

Clarkville
Louisville
Greenville
Lee's-town
Lexington
Bryans

LINCOLN

Harrods Town
Bards Town
Fine Cane

COUNTY   COUNTY

SALT   RIVER

GREEN   RIVER

CUMBERLAND   RIVER

HER MAJESTY'S STATE PAPER OFFICE

North-West Continent
of AMERICA
discover'd by Cap.t Cook.

Here according to the account of the Natives

Dog Rib Indians

Bear L.

Captain Cook found the water on this Coast to be much fresher
than Salt or Sea water, likewise a quantity of drift wood, no doubt
carried there by the Rivers Athabasca, Peace and Mountain, especially as
they annually overflow their banks in the months of May and August, the former
owing to the Ice breaking up, the latter to the great quantity of Snow upon the
Mountains where they take their source, melting at that time, and at each of
which these periods there drives down a large quantity of Wood, such as is not to be
met with to the Northward of the aforemention'd Rivers.

A broken Country
many Lakes & Rivers

a Great Water fall

GULF
of
ANADYR

T S C H U T S K I

East Cape

Tschutko-Noss

Cape Prince of Wales

Stuart I.

Norton Sound

Cape
Stevens

P.t Shallow
Water

S.t Thomas

S.t Titt

S.t Laurence

S.t Diomeas

S.t Andrean Islands

S.t Samuel

S.t Matheu

W E S T E R N

S.t Prednitsina

O C E A N

Shoal Ness

Cape Newenham

Broad B.

Sandwich Sound

Mt. S.t Elias

Hinchinbrooke I.

Cape S.t Elias

Cape Suckling

Cooks R.

Pike

Umanak

Unalaschca

13

Shumagins I.

P.t S.t Charles

Cape Providence

Cooks Track

N O R T H

P A C I F I

O C E A N

180

175

North America 1787

Left: This map illustrates the region of North America from Hudson's Bay and Lake Superior to the west coast and Alaska. Information provided includes place names, rivers, mountains, Indian tribes, notes on the country and military forts. Also illustrated is Captain James Cook's voyage through the north Pacific in 1778. Cook, a native of Whitby in the North Riding of Yorkshire, was one of Britain's foremost explorers in the late 18th century. Although eventually to be killed on one of his explorations, he was at the forefront of expanding British knowledge (and power) through the Pacific. Although this map, with its use of the latitude and longitude lines, looks as though it has more scientific authenticity to it, comparison with a more modern map reveals great inaccuracies. Note in particular the relative crudeness of Alaska. At this time, while the eastern seaboard had been well documented, explorers were only gradually piecing together information about the Pacific coastline.

MAP of the LANDS
around
The NORTH POLE
by
A. Dalrymple
1789.

Meridian of Greenwich

CHINA

ASIA

KOREA

YESO

AMERICA

UNITED STATES

LOUISIANA

NEW MEXICO

MEXICO

HUDSON'S BAY

BAFFIN'S BAY

GROENLAND

Davis Strait

FOX ISLANDS

KAMTCHATKA

KORIAKS

TSCHUTSKI

Hyperborean Sea

North America 1789

Left: This unusual perspective shows the lands around the North Pole. It was produced by A. Dalrymple and published on 4 May 1789. By this date, following the voyages of Bering and Cook, much more was known about North America's Pacific coastline, although there was still a great deal to be discovered about the interior of the continent to the west of the Rockies. The choice of perspective is interesting; one of the great imperatives for the exploration of North America was the belief in the presence of a North West Passage, which would provide easy access for European traders and sailors to the riches of India and the Far East.

Detroit 1792

Right: A plan of Fort Lernoult (L'Arnaud) and its frontage to the Detroit River; this map was included as an enclosure with correspondence filed by Lieutenant Governor Clarke on 5 September 1792. Located on the narrow waterway between lakes Huron and Erie, the name Detroit is French is origin ('détroit' meaning strait). The city's origins date back to 1701 when a fort was established by Antoine de la Mothe Cadillac. This was captured by the British in 1760 and remained in British hands until 1796 when it was captured by US forces after their victory at the Battle of Fallen Timber. Under the terms of the Treaty of Paris, which settled the American Revolutionary War, Britain was supposed to vacate the fort at Detroit and a number of other posts; using the fact that the American authorities had failed to fulfil certain obligations, Britain retained the posts and used them to divert the fur trade through to Canada, thus retaining an economic interest in the region. In the end, the forts would be taken from the British by force of arm.

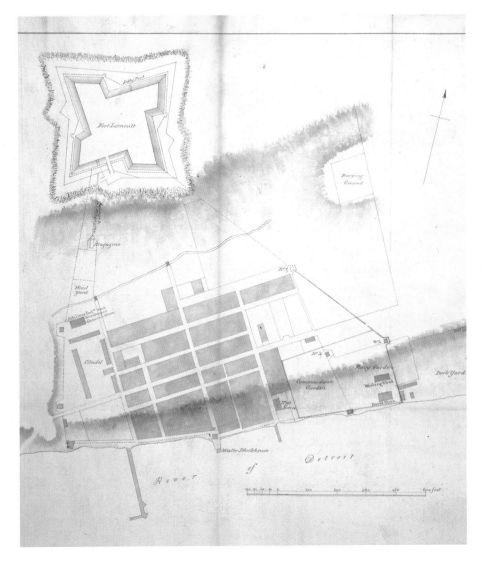

PLAN
of the City of Washington
in the Territory of Columbia.
ceded by the States of
VIRGINIA and MARYLAND
to the United States of America,
and by them established as the
SEAT of their GOVERNMENT,
after the Year
MDCCC.

Engrav'd by Sam.l Hill. Boston.

GEORGE TOWN.

Road leading from the Canal at the lower falls, distant 3¾ Miles.

HER MAJESTY'S STATE PAPER OFFICE.

Rock Creek.

Recdy Branch.

Tiber Creek.

above the level of the tide in said Creek...... 236..7..⅝

Perpendicular height of the West branch, above the tide in Tiber Creek........ 115.7..⅝ F. I. Pts.

The water of this Creek may be conveyed on the high Ground where the Capitol stands, and after watering that part of the City, may be destined to other useful purposes.

The perpendicular height of the ground where the Capitol is to stand, is above the tide of Tiber Creek, 78 feet.

Lat. ...
Long. ...

New Hampshire Avenue.
Massa...
Rhode Island.
Connecticut.
Vermont.
New York.
New Jersey.
North Capitol Street.
Delaware.
Pennsylvania.
President's House.
Mouth of Tiber Creek.
Capitol.
East Capitol Street.
Ma...
Virginia.
North Carolina.
South Carolina.
South Capitol Street.
North Carolina.

PART OF VIRGINIA WITHIN THE TERRITORY OF COLUMBIA.

POTOMAK RIVER.

EASTERN ...

MARYLAND ...

Observations
explanatory of the Plan.

I. THE positions for the different Edifices, and for the several Squares or Areas of different shapes, as they are laid down, were first determined on the most advantageous ground, commanding the most extensive prospects, and the better susceptible of such improvements as either use or Ornament may hereafter call for.

II. LINES or avenues of direct communication have been devised, to connect the separate and most distant objects with the principal, and to preserve through the whole a reciprocity of sight at the same time. Attention has been paid to the passing of those leading Avenues over the most favorable ground for prospect and convenience.

III. NORTH and South lines, intersected by others running ...

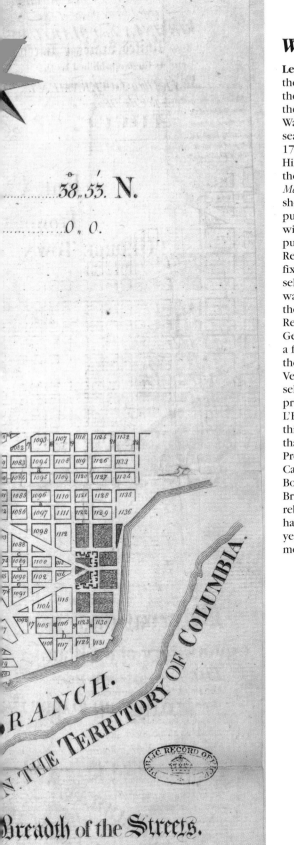

38,53. N.

0, 0.

1107 1118 1125 1132
1082
1093
9 1083 1094 1108 1119 1126 1133
1084 1095 1109 1120 1127 1134
1085 1096 1110 1121 1128 1135
1086 1097 1111 1122 1129 1136
1098 1112
1088 1100
74 1089 1100
1090 1102
74 1091
1104 1115
1002
7 1105 1116 1123 1130
100 1117 1124 1131
19

BRANCH.

IN THE TERRITORY OF COLUMBIA.

PUBLIC RECORD OFFICE

Breadth of the Streets.

Avenues, and such Streets as lead immediately to
130 to 160 feet wide, and may be conveniently divided.

Washington 1792

Left: Plan of the city of Washington in the Territory of Columbia. Ceded by the states of Virginia and Maryland to the United States of America, Washington was established as the seat of their government after the year 1790. This was engraved by Samuel Hill of Boston and appeared as part of the *Universal Asylum and Columbia Magazine* for March 1792. The map shows in detail the arrangement of public buildings and streets, along with the dimensions of the major public thoroughfares. After the Revolutionary War, the USA had no fixed capital until New York was selected in 1789; in 1790 New York was supplanted by Philadelphia but in the same year the Congress passed the Residence Act, which empowered George Washington to select a site for a federal capital. He chose an area on the Potomac River, close to Mount Vernon (his country house), and also selected Pierre-Charles L'Enfant to produce designs for the new city. It is L'Enfant's plans which are recorded in this map. Construction work meant that, by 1800, both Congress and the President were able to occupy the Capitol and White House respectively. Both buildings were destroyed by the British in 1814 but were subsequently rebuilt. It was not until the second half of the 19th century and the early years of the 20th that Washington was more fully completed.

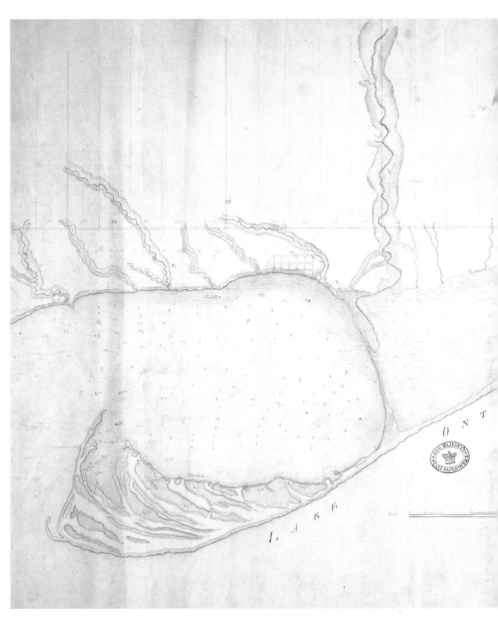

York 1793

Above: This is a plan of York Harbour (Toronto) on Lake Ontario in Canada which was surveyed on the orders of Lieutenant Governor Simcoe. The legend reads: A — proposed block house; B — proposed battery; C — proposed barracks; D — city of York; and, E — point from where view was taken. The scale is one inch to 20 chains. At this time, immediately after the American Revolutionary War, more than 100,000 loyalists from the 'Thirteen Colonies' had migrated north to Canada and the relations between the former British colonies and those territories which remained under British rule remained tense. The threat of war, particularly as Britain was at war with France (the USA's ally during the War of Independence) in Europe, meant that the threat of invasion had to be guarded against.

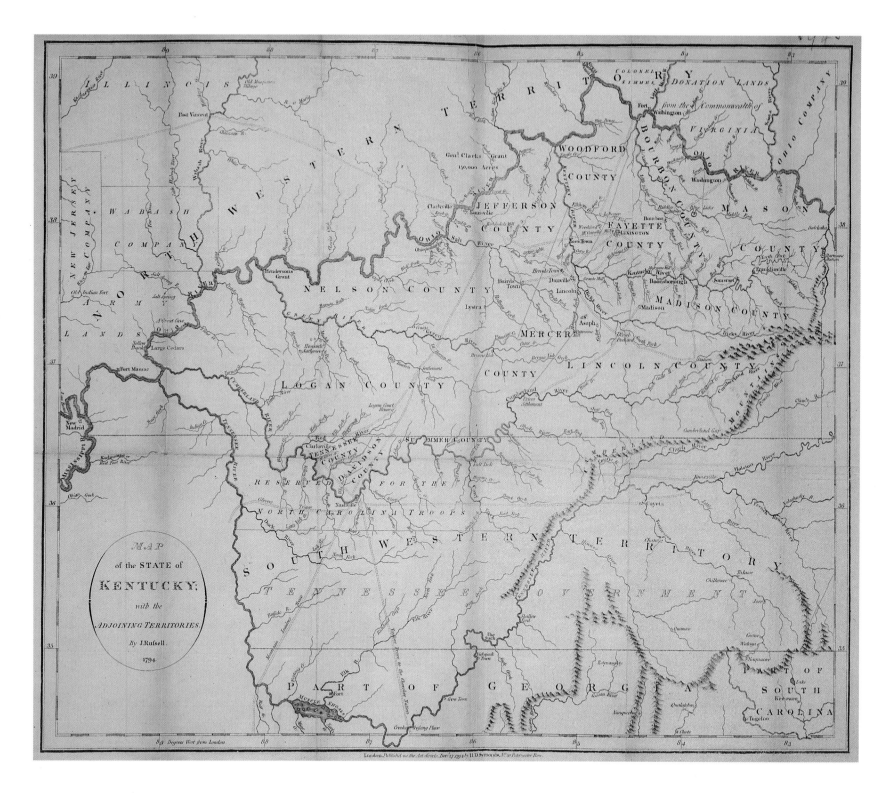

MAP of the STATE of KENTUCKY; with the ADJOINING TERRITORIES. By J. Russell. 1794

Kentucky 1794

Left: Published by H. D. Symonds of 20 Paternoster Row in London and drawn to a scale of about 23 miles to one inch, this is a map of the state of Kentucky and its adjoining territories. The original map was drawn by J. Russell. The name Kentucky is derived from the Native American phrase meaning 'land of tomorrow'. Kentucky was part of the great territory located to the west of the original colonies ceded to the new United States by Britain in 1783. The land, first settled by the British and French in the late 17th century, suffered from incursions from pro-British Indians during the War of Independence. The new state became the 15th member of the Union on 1 June 1792. Amongst the settlements of the state are Lexington, founded in 1781 and named after a notable battle of the War of Independence fought in Massachusetts, Harrodsburg, founded in 1774 and the oldest European settlement west of the Alleghenies, and Fort Knox, now famous as the home of the US gold reserves.

Maine 1798

Right: Described as 'Maine entworfen von D. F. Sotzmann. Hamburg bey Carl Ernst Bohn 1798', this map, drawn to a scale of 16 miles to one inch, shows land grants in each county. There is a reference table that details grants, stage coach and post routes. The gradual carving up of each individual state into smaller land grants was an essential part of the evolution of the US landscape. At the time that this map was drawn, the northern boundary of the state was still ill-defined; it would not be finally settled until agreement with the British in 1842.

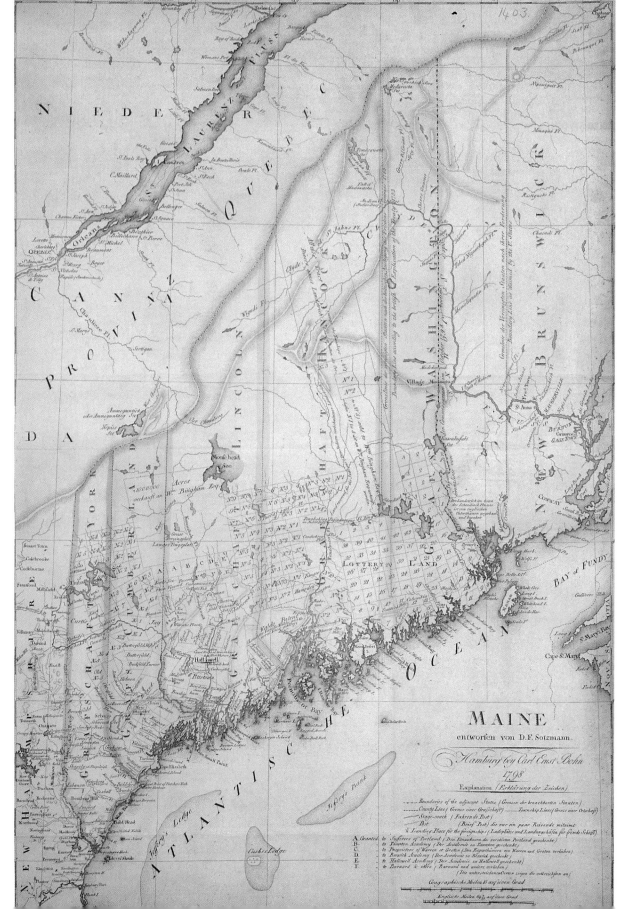

Vermont 1798

Above right: A map of the state of Vermont drawn under the direction of Ira Allen, Esq, late Surveyor General of the state, for inclusion in his history of the state. The map was published in London on 28 March 1798 and formed an enclosure to a letter sent by a Colonel Tatham on 19 April of the same year. The area was first investigated by Europeans at the start of the 17th century, when Samuel de Champlain, the Frenchman who founded Quebec, traversed the region, discovering the lake which still bears his name. European settlement began in the early 18th century, but in the period of colonial rule the region formed a single province with New Hampshire. The border today runs along the Connecticut River. In 1777 Vermont adopted its own constitution, and was the first of the future United States to ban slavery. Vermont was admitted to the Union at the 14th state — the first after the original 'Thirteen Colonies' — on 4 March 1791.

Virgin Islands c1800

Below right: Located to the east of Puerto Rico, the Virgin Islands were, at the time of this map, colonised by the British and by the Danes. Drawn by George King, land surveyor of the British part of the island group, this map shows the British possessions and the sailing lanes between the various islands. One of the major imperatives for map makers at the time was the need for good charts for sailing; the dangers that these waters could cause to unwary sailors is evinced by the fact that more than 400 ships are believed to have been shipwrecked off Anageda since the islands were first discovered. The largest island is Tortola with an area of 21sq miles. With the exception of Anegada, which is flat and made of coral, the British islands are hilly, rising to 1,780ft above sea level. The United States acquired the Danish Virgin Islands for $25 million on 25 January 1917. The British Virgin Islands remain a British territory.

Canada 1800

Far right: 'A map of the Province of upper Canada describing all the new settlements and townships with the counties adjacent from Quebec to Lake Huron compiled at the request of his excellency Major General John G. Simcoe, first Lieutenant General, by David William Smyth, Surveyor General, and published by W. Faden at Charing Cross in London on 12 April 1800.' Note that part of Lake Huron is annotated with the comment 'Erroneously laid down' and that the map also shows the course of a proposed road from Amhurstburg and Kingston via York (Toronto).

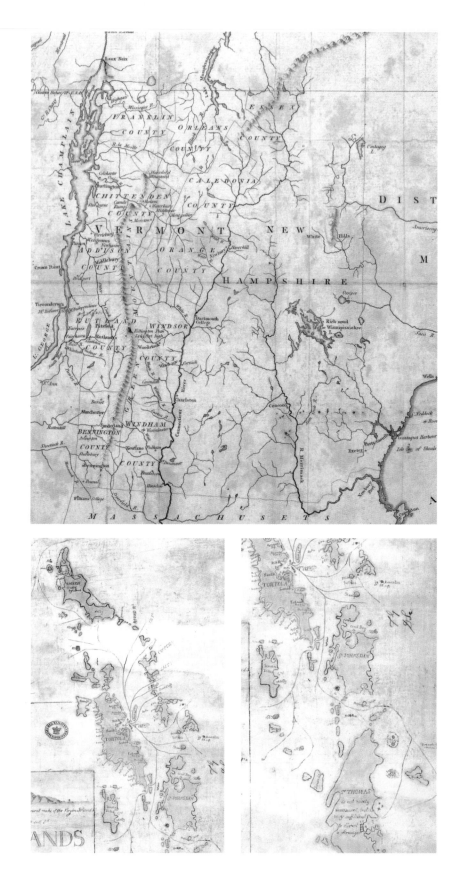

North America 1803

Left and Below (detail): Published by W. Faden, Cartographer to the King (George III) and to the Prince of Wales (the future George IV), at Charing Cross, London, in 1809, this map shows the lands occupied by the Spanish, the United States and the British. It is interesting to note that the map refers to the 'United States of North America'. The map is colour-coded, with red being British territory, yellow being United States', green being Spanish, purple for Native American territory and blue being allocated to the French fishing rights off Newfoundland. The map is annotated with two interesting additional comments. The first states 'The whole of the countries not actually settled by Europeans should belong by right to the Aborigines [Native Americans] but our intention has been only to indicate the few limits that are known of their respective possessions as well as the boundaries of the lands granted by them or those with the several states to which they have agreed'. The second, reflecting that the Spanish still controlled Florida, states 'The British denomination of East and West Florida has been retained, although we are not certain that it is adopted by the Spaniards'.

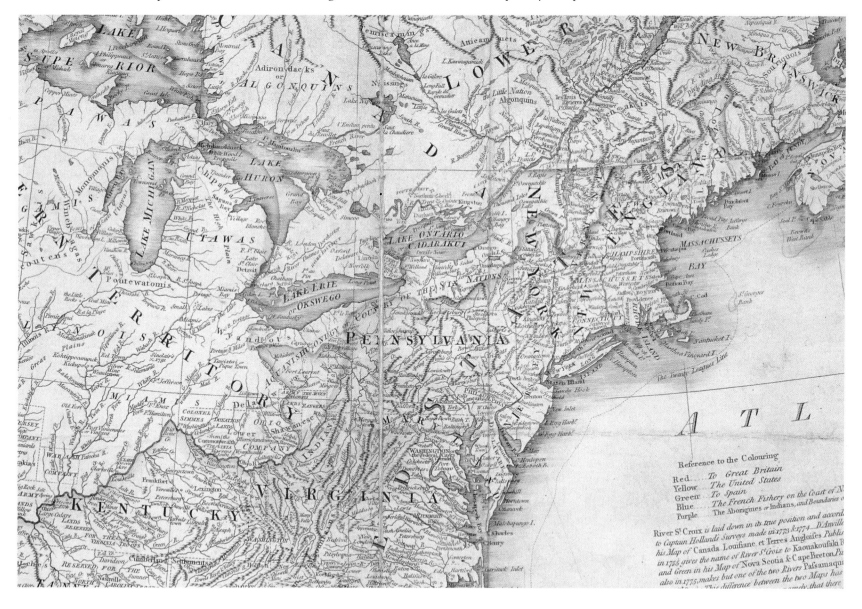

St Croix 1809

Above: This is a map of the Danish island of St Croix in the West Indies. It was originally surveyed by P. L. Oxholm in 1799 and republished by W. Faden in London on 1 March 1809. Apart from the actual map, the tabular information provided gives a fascinating insight into the size of population and the nature of the island's trades at the start of the 19th century. According to the figures given, there were 2,223 whites, 1,164 coloured and 25,452 negroes on St Croix at the time and these produced 18,714,000lb of sugar, 838,100 gallons of rum and 12,600lb of cotton per annum. In terms of infrastructure, the island possessed no fewer than 115 windmills. St Croix was the southernmost of the Danish Virgin Islands and would be sold to the United States of America in 1917.

Eastern United States 1809

Right: Described as 'A New Chart of the Coast of North America from New York to Cape Hatteras including the Bays of Delaware and Chesapeak [sic], with the Coasts of New Jersey, Maryland, Virginia and part of the Coast of North Carolina', this map was drawn originally by Capt N. Holland and was published in this 'improved version' by Laurie and Whittle of 53 Fleet Street, London on 12 May 1809. Drawn to a scale of about 10 nautical miles to one inch, the map also includes silhouettes of the coasts near Cape Henry and of Sandy Hook lighthouse as well as a table of astronomical observations. The period from which this map dates was one when increasing tension between Britain and the United States would ultimately lead to the 1812 war. Britain and France were again at war in Europe and neither country showed any real inclination to respect US neutrality and on 22 December 1807 the US Congress passed the Embargo Act, which theoretically banned the US from trading with the European combatants. It was an unpopular measure domestically, as US traders lost potentially lucrative business whilst it also proved almost impossible to police. In 1809 the Embargo Act was repealed and replaced by the Non-Intercourse Act, which permitted trade with European nations except Britain and France unless the latter announced respect for neutral shipping. The British representative, David M. Erskine, agreed to these terms and shipping between the USA and Britain resumed; unfortunately, Erskine had been acting without authorisation with the result that the Royal Navy began to seize US-flagged ships again. The result was that anti-British feeling grew, culminating on 1 June 1812 with a declaration of war. Ironically, by 1812 tension between Britain and the USA was in decline, but the anti-British element within Congress held sway. The date of this map is, therefore, significant, in that it is contemporaneous with the maritime dispute between Britain and the USA and shows the preparedness of the Royal Navy for action against shipping emanating from US ports.

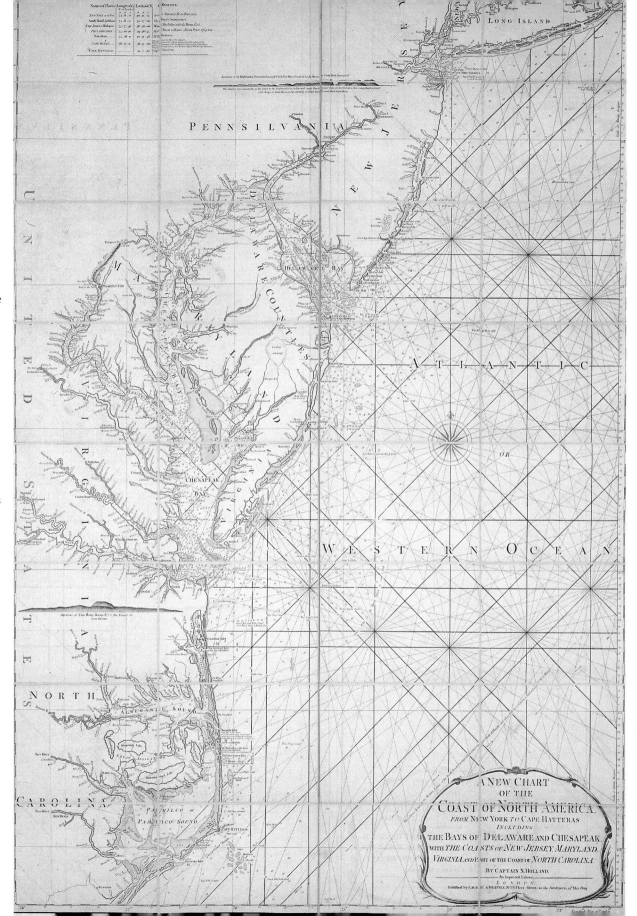

United States 1813

Right and Far Right: Published by John Melish of Philadelphia in March 1813, these two maps show the constituent states and territories of the United States of America along with the adjoining British and Spanish territories at the time of the War of 1812. Each map includes a table giving the population of the states and major towns illustrated. Note that the border between Maine and New Brunswick was at this time delineated, but still not finalised and that in the south, the British division of Florida into West and East was perpetuated, even though the territory was again in Spanish hands. Note also that the 15th (Kentucky), 16th (Tennessee), 17th (Ohio) and 18th (Louisiana) states of the Union are not described as territories, unlike those areas, such as Mississippi, which had yet to achieve statehood. The War of 1812 was arguably one of the most unnecessary in history, but resulted from Britain's naval blockade of France during the Napoleonic wars. American merchant shipping and trade suffered and, during 1807–9, the United States under President Jefferson imposed a trade embargo on Britain. This however, failed and further deterioration in relations between the two nations led to the United States declaring war in 1812. Untrained US forces attacked the British in Canada and a series of battles were fought in the area of the Great Lakes; these battles, with neither side achieving dominance, gained neither the United States nor the British forces a great advantage. However, toward the end of the war, British forces swept southwards from Lake Champlain and captured Washington, destroying the White House in August 1814. A British attempt to land forces at New Orleans was soundly defeated by US forces under Andrew Jackson.

MAP of the Seat of War in NORTH AMERICA.

TABLE of POPULATION

United States	7. 239. 903
British Pofsefsions	330. 000

Comparative Population along the Lines

Maine	228. 705	
New Hampshire	214. 460	
Vermont	217. 895	
New York	959. 049	
Pennsylvania	810. 091	
Ohio	230. 760	
Michigan Territory	4. 762	2. 665. 722
Nova Scotia	about	40. 000
New Brunswick	do.	45. 000
Lower Canada	do.	150. 000
Upper Canada	do.	80. 000	315. 000
Halifax		8. 000
Quebec		12. 000
Montreal		20. 000
Newark		500
Queenstown		300
Malden		500

J. Melish, del.   H.S. Tanner, Dirext.

10 20 30 40 50 60 70 80 90 100 Miles

Delaware 1813

Right: Published by John Melish of Philadelphia in 1813, this shows the Atlantic coast of the United States from Lynhaven Bay to Narraganset Bay. Of particular interest is the table which gives the population sizes of the major towns and cities within the region covered. Note that at this date New York had a population of 96,373 but Philadelphia was larger, with some 111,210. Delaware, at the centre of this map, was first settled by the Swedes in 1638 but later fell under Dutch control. Following the British take-over in 1664, Delaware became part of Pennsylvania in 1682. It became an independent colony again in 1775 and was to become the first state to ratify the new constitution of the USA on 7 December 1787.

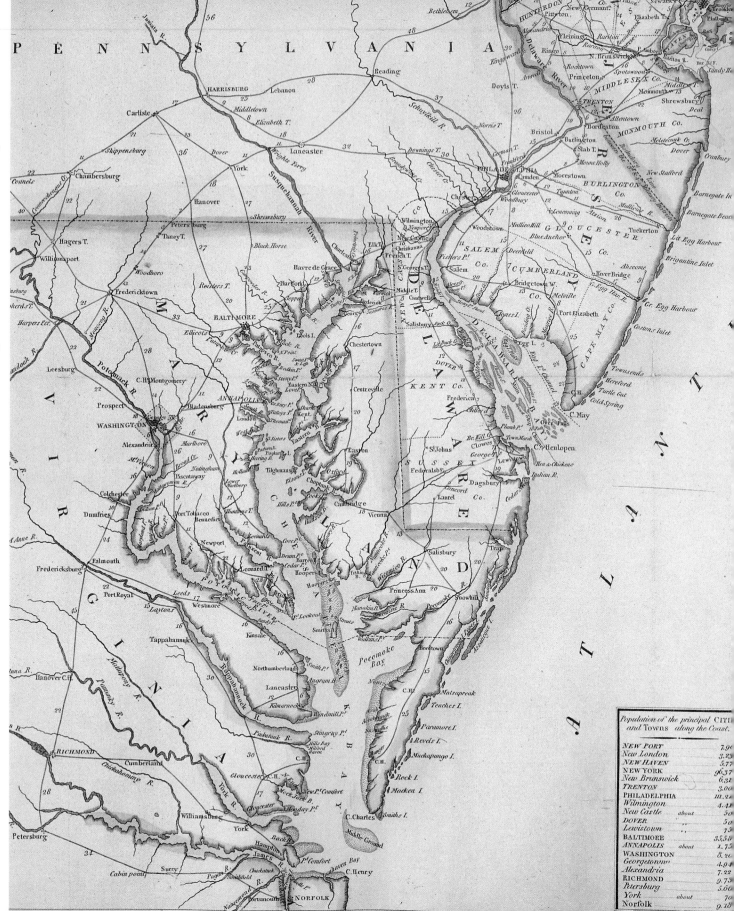

Population of the principal CITIES and Towns along the Coast.	
NEW PORT	7,9
New London	3,2
NEW HAVEN	5,7
NEW YORK	96,37
New Brunswick	6,3
TRENTON	3,0
PHILADELPHIA	111,2
Wilmington	4,4
New Castle about	5
DOVER	5
Lewistown	1,
BALTIMORE	35,5
ANNAPOLIS about	1,7
WASHINGTON	8,2
Georgetown	4,9
Alexandria	7,2
RICHMOND	9,7
Petersburg	
York about	7
Norfolk	9,1

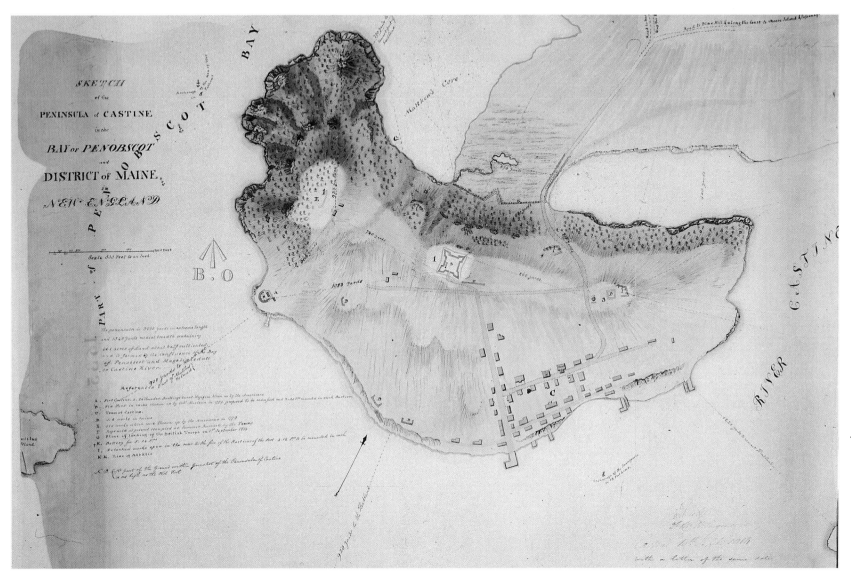

Castine 1814

Above: This is a sketch of the Peninsula of Castine in the Bay of Penobscot in Maine and shows the landing of British troops on 1 September 1814. It was drawn by Capt R. H. Bonnycastle of the Royal Engineers on behalf of Lt-Col G. Nicholls, also of the Royal Engineers, on 10 September and sent by the latter to accompany a letter of the same date to Gen. Mann. Drawn to a scale of 500ft to one inch, the reference table gives details of defence works, buildings and the landing place of troops. The British-American War of 1812 and after, was the result of anti-British sentiment in Congress and a feeling that Britain could be forced to concede to US demands for maritime rights by starving British colonies in the Caribbean through conquest of Canada. At the time, Britain was involved in the war against Napoleonic France and, therefore, the timing might have been propitious for the militarily weak US forces. However, the US invasion of Canada — half-hearted at best — was unsuccessful and, more importantly was ill timed as war in Europe was gradually moving in favour of Britain and its allies. By 1814, with Napoleon temporarily incarcerated, Britain was able to turn its attention to North America. As part of the British tactics, a number of raiding parties were landed on the east coast of the USA, linked into a naval blockade of the ports, and this map records one of these incursions. It followed on from the successful landing further south, in August, when the British captured Washington and preceded a less successful assault on Baltimore on 14 September when the defending forces beat off the attack.

Battle of Bladensburg 1814

Right and Below (detail): Drawn to a scale of quarter of a mile to one inch, this sketch portrays the engagement that occurred on 24 August 1814 between British and American troops at Bladensburg, in Maryland. The map includes a detailed key outlining the location of the opposing forces. The town of Bladensburg is just to the east of Washington, DC, and, as described on page 112, the British reaction to the American declaration of war in 1812, was during 1814, to undertake a naval blockade of the eastern seaboard and land raiding parties at strategic locations. The engagement recorded here was part of the successful British raid that was to lead, on the same day, to the capture of Washington itself and the destruction of the original White House and Capitol.

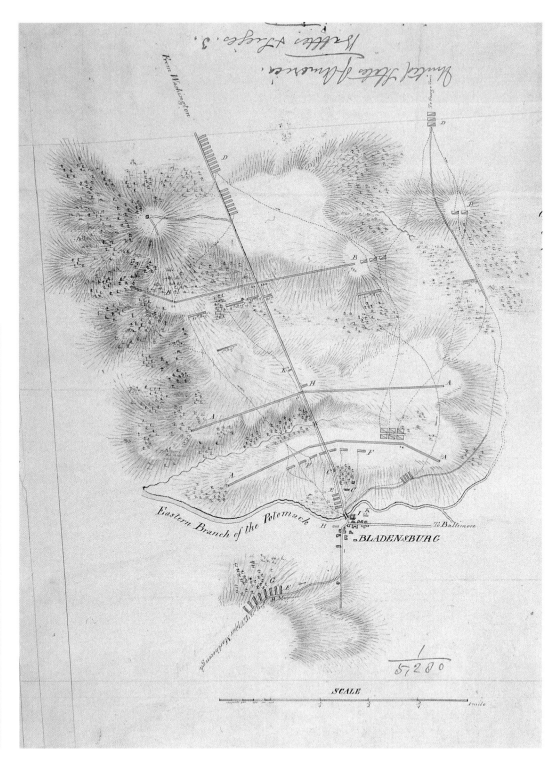

SKETCH

Of the Engagement on the 24th
of August 1814 between the
British and American Forces.
at Bladensburg. 1814.

A A. 1st Position of the Enemy

B B. 2nd Position of Do.

C C. Enemy's Guns Enfilading the road.

D D. Enemys Cavalry and Infantry retreating

E E. British Columns advancing

F F. Skirmishers covering the Columns

G 2nd Brigade

H H. Rocket Brigade

NB. The Arrows denote the direction of the Movement

I. Fortified house abandoned by the enemy

K. British Artillery

New Orleans 1815

Right: This sequence of three maps illustrates the military engagement between British and American forces at New Orleans in the period from 23 December 1814 to 8 January 1815. This battle was one of the most important fought during the War of 1812; ironically, however, the engagement took place after the Treaty of Ghent (December 1814) had settled the war, but such was the slowness in getting the information to North America that the battle took place. In an age dominated by electronic media, it is very easy to forget that this revolution in the transmission of news only really started in the mid-19th century with the development of Morse.

The first of the three maps — described as a sketch of the position of the British and American forces — illustrates various phases in the battle and was compiled by John Pedder.
A. The enemy's position on the night of 23 December.
B. Bivouac for the troops on 23 December.
C. Position on the night of 23 December.
D. Position on the night of 24 December.
E. Position after the advance of 28 December.
F. Colonel Thompson's attack on morning of 8 January.
G. Colonel Thornton's furthest advance
1-8. Redoubts built after advance of 28 December.
H. The enemy retiring.

The second map, in water-colour and ink by Lt Thomas Campbell, illustrates some of the military hardware available:
1. Four 18-pounders
2. Two 8in howitzers
3. Two six-pounders
4. Three 5.5in mortars and three 4.4in mortars
5/6. Advanced trucks on the right of the 10th.

The final map shows the groundplan and sections of the fort at New Orleans. It was compiled by Charles R. Scott of the Royal Staff Corps.
The battle at New Orleans was part of an abortive effort by British forces to invade the USA; in the event the attack was repulsed by US forces under General Andrew Jackson.

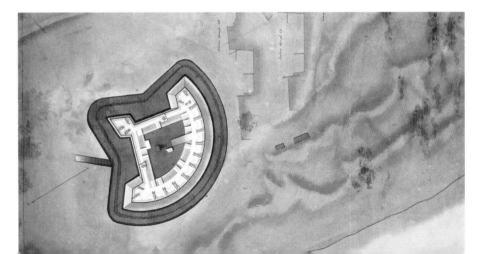

North America 1824

Right, Below and to page 122: This series of detail maps, which has been produced from the single and much larger map (**Right**), shows the extent of knowledge of North America. Published in London by James Wyld, successor to W. Faden at Charing Cross as cartographer to the King (King George IV) and to the Duke of York, on 1 May 1824. It cites its various sources and shows clearly the Spanish possessions as well as those of Britain and the USA. The map was produced shortly after the US acquisition of Florida (in 1819) but before the conflict of the 1840s which saw the US acquire Texas, California, New Mexico, etc. By this date, Spanish power in the region had declined significantly and much of central America was now — from 1821 — the independent state of Mexico. Cuba, however, remained a Spanish possession

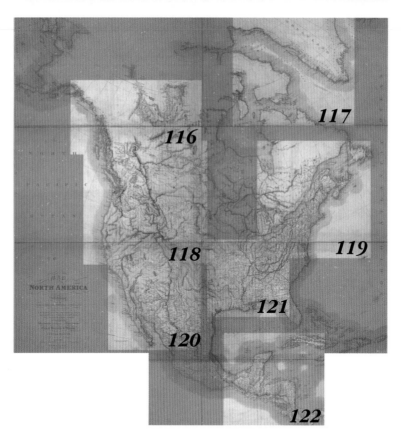

Left: Light areas in this composite map indicate sections which are displayed on the following pages.

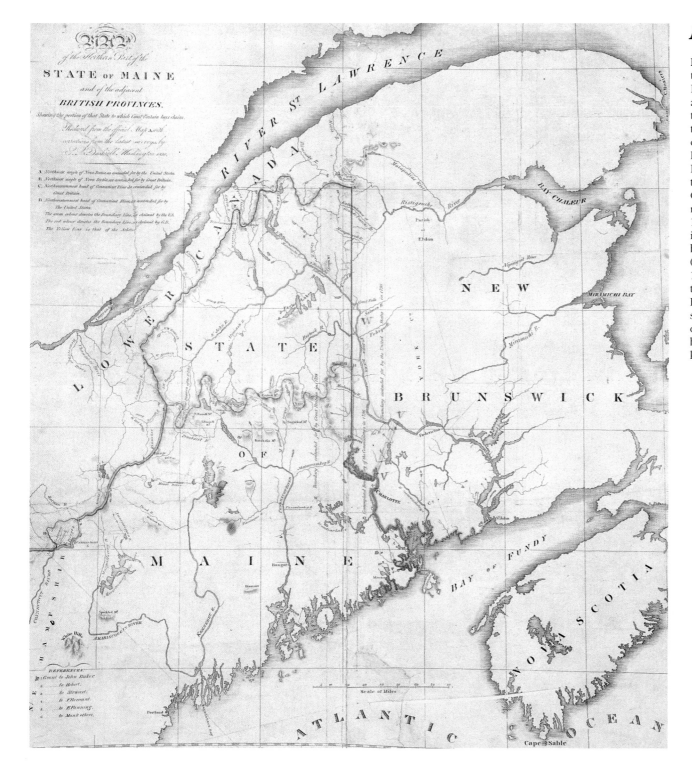

Maine 1830

Left: This is a map of the northern part of the state of Maine and of the adjacent British provinces — now New Brunswick and Quebec — showing that portion of the state which Britain still claimed, with the various contentious areas clearly delineated. The map was drawn by S. L. Dashiell, of Washington, and engraved by B. Chambers, also of Washington. Despite the war of 1812/13 and the Treaty of Ghent of 24 December 1814, which reconfirmed the borders as agreed in 1783, there remained a number of territorial disputes. One of these concerned the border between Maine and Lower Canada (Quebec)/New Brunswick. In the early 1830s arbitration over the disputed territory was undertaken by the King of Holland. The territorial dispute was finally settled with the Webster-Ashburton Treaty of 1842, which effectively drew the boundary along the line suggested in the king's arbitration.

Nebraska, Arkansas and Oklahoma 1833

Below: A map of the western territory drawn to a scale of 50 miles to one inch. The map illustrates the Indian tribal territories and their boundaries with the USA. There is a reference to 'This tract has not yet been granted to the Cherokees, but provision has been made for ceding it to them by a treaty now awaiting the action of the President and the Senate'. Arkansas was first explored by a European when a Spaniard, Hernando de Soto, travelled through the region in 1541. By the 17th century, the future state had fallen under French influence, but was to passed to Spain in 1763. It was regained by France in 1799 before being sold to the USA as part of the Louisiana Purchase in 1803. Arkansas became the 25th state of the Union on 15 June 1836. The area today known as Nebraska became part of the French colony of Louisiana in 1682, passing to United States' control in 1803. It was to become the 37th state on 1 March 1867. Like Arkansas, the future Oklahoma was first investigated by the Spaniards in 1541. it became part of Louisiana in 1682, again forming part of the Louisiana Purchase of 1803. Deemed by the US authorities to be land of no value, the area was designated as a reserve for the Indian (Chickasaw, Cherokee, Choctaw, Creek and Seminole) tribes. The allocation of land in this map is a reflection of this policy, which saw the Indians driven from their traditional lands further east. In 1889, the US government allowed for the white settlement of the region and on 16 November 1907 Oklahoma became the 46th state of the Union.

Wisconsin 1836

Right: A map of the territory of Wisconsin by David H. Burr, Draftsman to the House of Representatives, to accompany the Hon Z. Casey's report. The area covered includes the area in Iowa ceded by the Sioux, Sac and Fox Indians of 15 July 1830. Wisconsin's name is derived from the Indian word meaning 'where the waters meet'. The map is also of interest in that it illustrates the route of a number of proposed military roads and railways. Given that the first generally accepted railway, the Stockton & Darlington, only opened in England in 1825 and that 1830 was the year that the more famous Liverpool & Manchester Railway opened, the extent of the proposed railways in this area of the USA is impressive and illustrates how quickly technology could be transferred. The state of Wisconsin was the 30th state of the Union, ratifying the constitution on 29 May 1848. The first European to reach the region was a Frenchman, Jean Nicolet, in 1634 and the area remained French until ceded to Britain after the Treaty of Paris in 1763. After the second Treaty of Paris in 1783, the area was nominally under US control, but Britain did not actually relinquish the land until after the War of 1812.

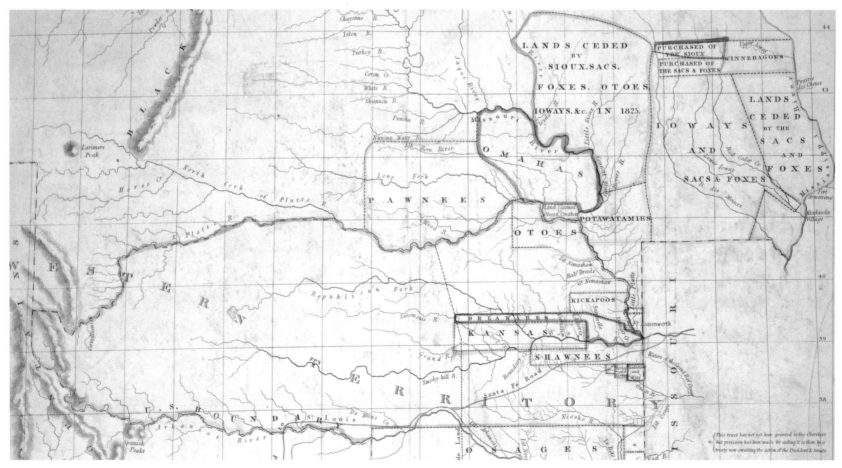

Indiana 1836

Left: This is a tourist's pocket map of the state of Indiana compiled by
J. H. Young of Philadelphia and published by S. Augustus Mitchell in 1836. Apart
from showing the state, the map includes tabular information which gives the
population county by county. This territory was first explored in the late 17th
century by the Frenchman, Sieur de la Salle. As with so much of French-controlled North America it passed to British rule in 1763 after the Treaty of Paris.
Becoming part of the independent United States in 1783, Indiana was originally
part of the large Northwest Territory; it became a separate territory in 1809 and
the 19th state of the Union on 11 December 1816. The local Indian tribe, the
Shawnee, were defeated at the battle of Tippecanoe on 7 November 1811; the
action was undertaken against the local Indians because the US authorities felt
that British agents from Canada were using the Indians as a means of preventing
the westward expansion of white settlement.

St Louis 1837

Above right: This is a map of the harbour of St Louis, on the Mississippi,
surveyed by Lt R. E. Lee, Corps of Engineers, assisted by Lt M. C. Meigs of the
Corps of Engineers, and by Messrs J. S. Morehead and H. Kayser. It was drawn
by Lt Meigs originally and later copied by M. C. Ewing, Civil Engineer, and
lithographed by W. J. Stone, Washington. The scale is 5in to one mile, with the
soundings of the river calculated in feet. St Louis owed its origins to the
establishment of a trading post in 1764 by a French fur trader, Pierre Laclède, and
named after an historic French King, Louis IX, who had been canonised. After the
Louisiana Purchase of 1803 it passed to US control and was to become increasingly important as a city through which setters passed on their way west. The
town of St Louis, as illustrated here, was largely destroyed in a major fire in 1849.
Robert E. Lee was to achieve greater fame as Commander-in-Chief of the
Confederate forces during the American Civil War.

Michigan 1843

Below right: A map of the surveyed part of Michigan by John Farmer. This map
was engraved by S. Stiles & Co and published in New York by J. H. Cotton. French
influence was to the fore in the development of the area later known as
Michigan. Traders, in particular those dealing in fur, reached the region in the
early 17th century, where they had dealings with the local Algonquin Indians. The
first permanent European settlement was established St Sault Ste Marie in 1686.
Following the Treaty of Paris in 1763, the region passed to British rule, before
forming part of the Northwest Territory on independence. It became a separate
territory in 1805 and, after a brief British occupation during the War of 1812, was
to become the 26th state of the Union on 26 January 1837.

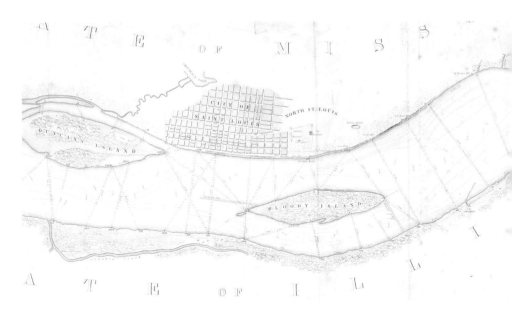

Pennsylvania 1843

Right: By the mid-19th century, Pennsylvania had grown into one of the most important states of the Union in economic terms. The presence of anthracite in the Appalachian Mountains meant that Pennsylvania was to develop as a major industrial state, with iron and steel predominating. Much of this heavy industry was concentrated around Pittsburgh — located close to the former French fort at Duquesne — and, with the increasing demands of the railway industry, as well as the munitions industry during the Civil War, Pittsburgh grew dramatically. Towards the end of the 1840s, following the failure of revolutions in various European countries, Philadelphia was to become home to a large number of German immigrants, whilst a sizeable black population was also to migrate to the region following the north's rejection of slavery.

United States 1843

Far right: This is a detail from Mitchell's National Map of the American Republic or United States of North America. At this time the USA consisted of the original 'Thirteen Colonies', the various states which had been created after 1783 (from Vermont in 1791 through to Arkansas in 1836) as well as the remainder of the territories acquired as part of the Louisiana Purchase in 1803 and those acquired from Spain in 1819. The former Spanish-controlled regions, which were under Mexican rule at this time, were not to be gained by the USA until later in this decade.

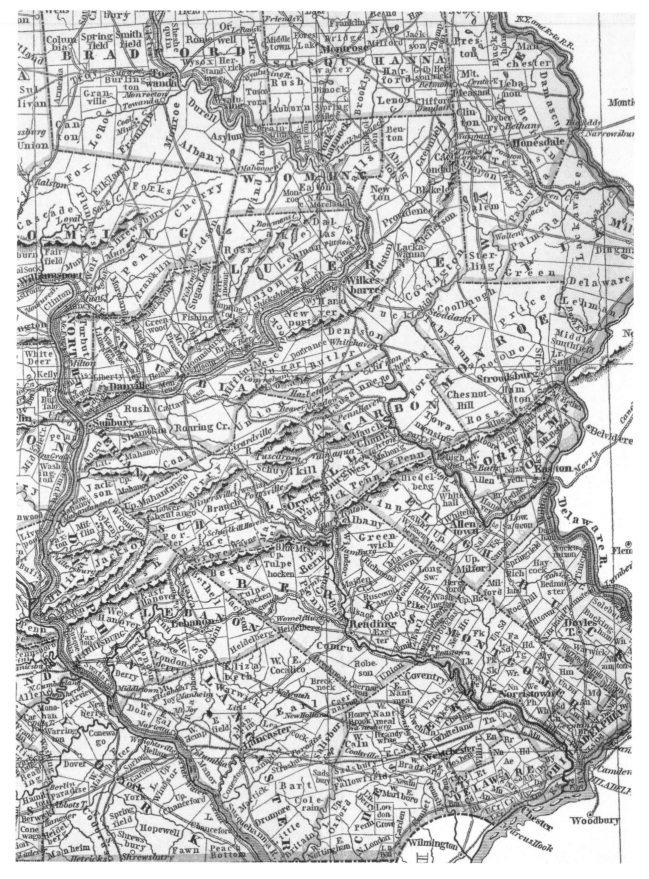

Illinois 1844

Left: A new sectional map of the state of Illinois compiled from the US surveys; this map also shows the internal improvements, distances between towns, etc. It was compiled by J. M. Peck, John Messinger and A. J. Mathewson and published by J. H. Cotton in New York. Two insets show the vicinity of Alton, St Louis and Galena. Illinois gains its name from the local Indian tribe which was first encountered by Europeans during the 17th century. In 1680 French control was exercised by the construction of the first fort on the site of the modern Peoria by Sieur de la Salle. After the Treaty of Paris in 1763, the region passed to British control but was captured by the Americans during the Revolutionary War in 1778. Illinois became the 21st state of the Union on 3 December 1818. By the date of this map, the local Indians had been subjugated through the Black Hawk War of 1832.

St John's 1844

Above right: In 1862 an Anglo-American Fishery Commission examined the state of the fishing industry within the coastal waters of North America. Some of the charts used were proprietary maritime charts altered with information derived from the commission, others were drawn specially for the commission. Each of the maps used were signed by the commissioners and were then bound into volumes held by the respective governments. St John's was one of the primary fishing ports on Newfoundland and had been captured by the British in 1708 during the War of Spanish Succession. The settlement of that war, the Treaty of Utrecht in 1713, ceded the whole of Newfoundland to Britain and Newfoundland was to remain a separate colony until it was incorporated into the Canadian Confederation on 1 April 1949.

New York 1845

Below right: Although initially overshadowed by Philadelphia, by the mid-19th century New York was rapidly growing and by 1820 it was the largest city in the United States with a population in excess of 150,000; its growth thereafter continued and, by 1913, the population exceeded five million. This map shows New York with an inset showing the city of New York along with parts of Brooklyn and Williamsburg. Brooklyn is today the largest of New York's boroughs; at the time that this map was compiled, none of the various bridges linking Brooklyn with Manhattan over the East River had been constructed. The first to be completed was the Brooklyn Bridge, a 1,150yd long suspension bridge, which was constructed between 1867 and 1883. Although the first Europeans to visit the future New York were an Italian (Giovanni de Verrazano) in 1524 and an Englishman working for the Dutch (Henry Hudson) in 1609, the first settlement was not established until 1626 when the peninsula was acquired by Peter Minuit from the Manna-Hatta Indians for 60 guilders worth of trinkets.

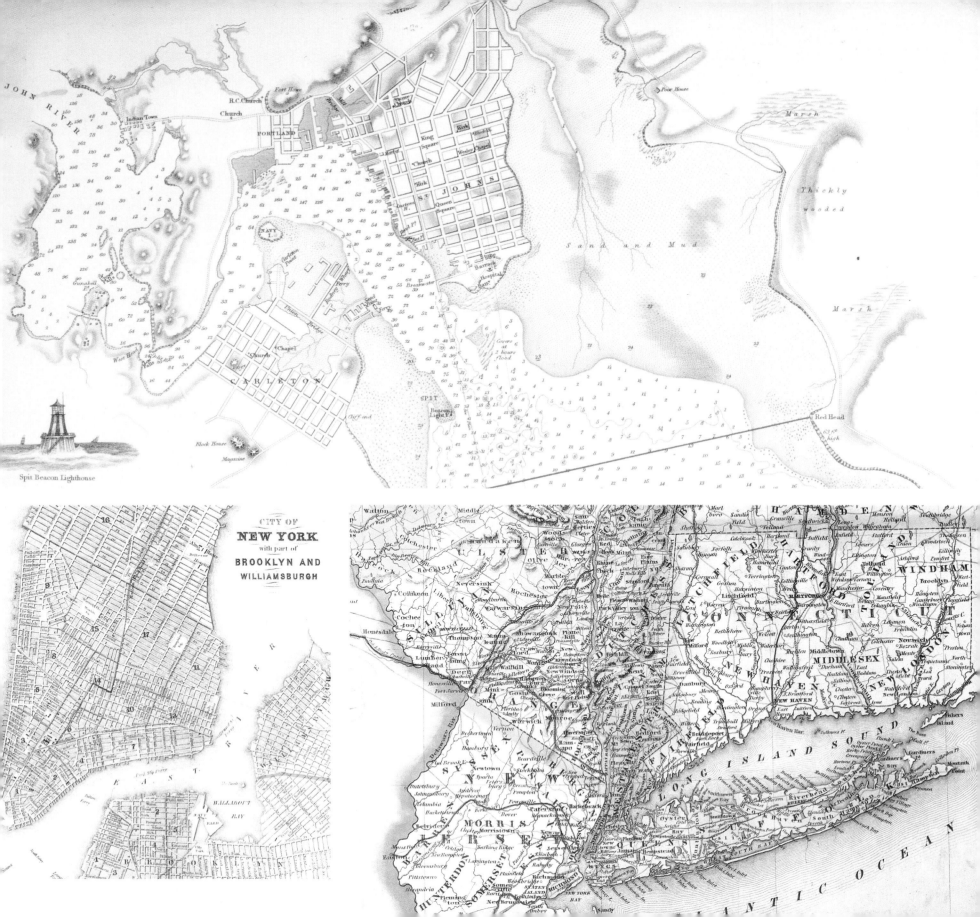

MAP OF

TEXAS

AND THE COUNTRIES ADJACENT

COMPILED IN THE BUREAU OF THE CORPS OF TOPOGRAPHICAL ENGINEERS
FROM THE BEST AUTHORITIES

FOR THE STATE DEPARTMENT

Under the direction of Colonel J. J. Abert Chief of the Corps
by W. H. Emory, 1st Lieut: T.E.

WAR DEPARTMENT
1844.

Texas 1844

Left: 'A map of Texas and the countries adjacent compiled in the bureau of the Corps of Topographical Engineers from the best authorities for the State Department under the direction of Colonel J. J. Abert, Chief of the Corps, by W. H. Emory, 1st Lt TE.' The map, produced to a scale of 70 miles to one inch, also includes a comprehensive list of sources from which Emory had produced this map. The date of the map is significant because, at the time of its compilation, Texas was an independent state. It was only to join the Union, as the 28th state on 29 December 1845. This was to lead to war between the United States and Mexico; it was the Treaty of Guadalupe Hidalgo of 1848, which settled the war and which also delineated the border between the USA and Mexico. Historically, Texas had fallen within the Spanish sphere of influence. The coastline had been first discovered by Alonson Alvarez de Piñeda in 1519 and nine years later, in 1528, Alvar Núñez Cabez de Vaca explored the interior after having been shipwrecked. Permanent settlements were established during the 17th century and, following the Mexican revolution in the early 19th century, Texas formed part of the independent Mexico in 1821. However, English-speaking settlers, led by Stephen and Moses Austin, rebelled against their Mexican masters and established the independent Texas in 1835.

Ohio 1845

Right Drawn by H. S. Taneer this is a map of Ohio showing its canals, roads and distances. There is also an inset plan of Cincinnati and a profile of the Ohio Canal. Another of the states that formed the Northwest Territory after Independence, Ohio was to achieve statehood on 1 March 1803 as the 17th state of the Union after the local Indians had been subjugated. The region had originally been colonised by the French, passing to the British after the Treaty of Paris in 1763. Cincinnati was one of the first white settlements to be established in the future state, being founded in 1788, after the defeat of the local Iroquois Indians. Its name was a tribute to the Roman general Cincinnatus. Located on the navigable Ohio River, Cincinnati was to become a vitally important regional centre for the development of the Mid-West.

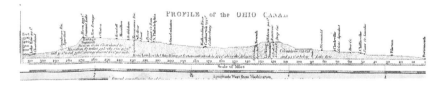

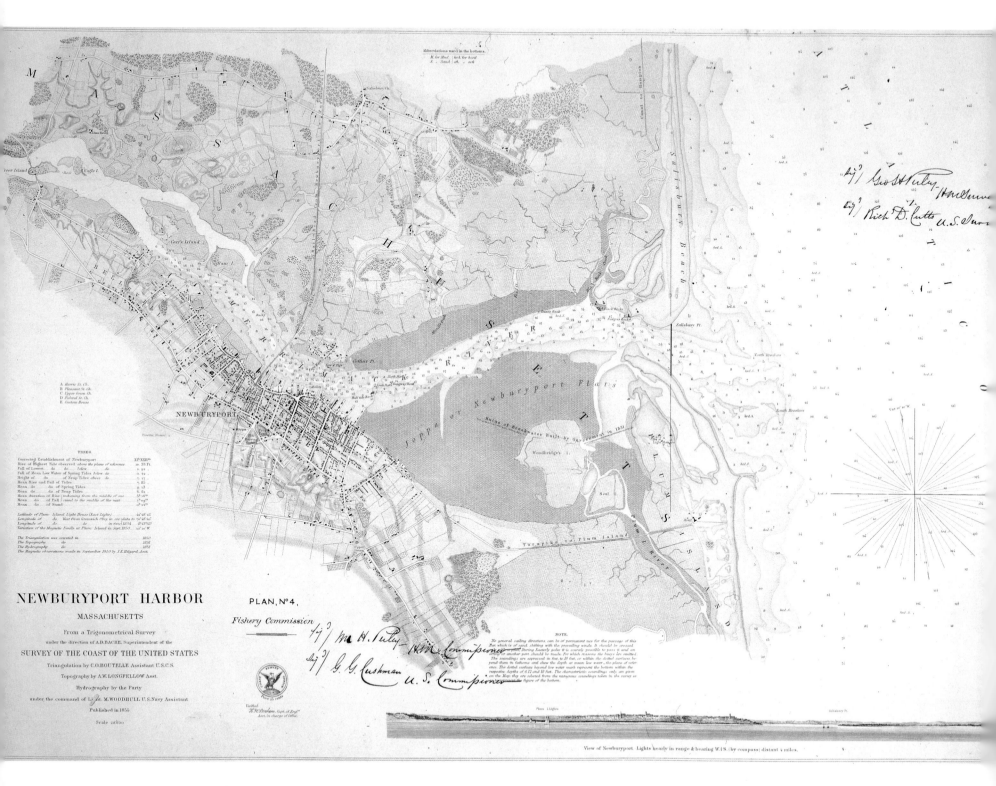

NEWBURYPORT HARBOR

MASSACHUSETTS

From a Trigonometrical Survey

under the direction of A.D.BACHE, Superintendent of the

SURVEY OF THE COAST OF THE UNITED STATES

Triangulation by C.O.BOUTELLE Assistant U.S.C.S.

Topography by A.W.LONGFELLOW Asst.

Hydrography by the Party

under the command of Lieut. M.WOODHULL U.S. Navy Assistant

Published in 1855

Scale 20000

PLAN, N° 4,

Fishery Commission

View of Newburyport. Lights nearly in range & bearing W.↓S. (by compass) distant 4 miles.

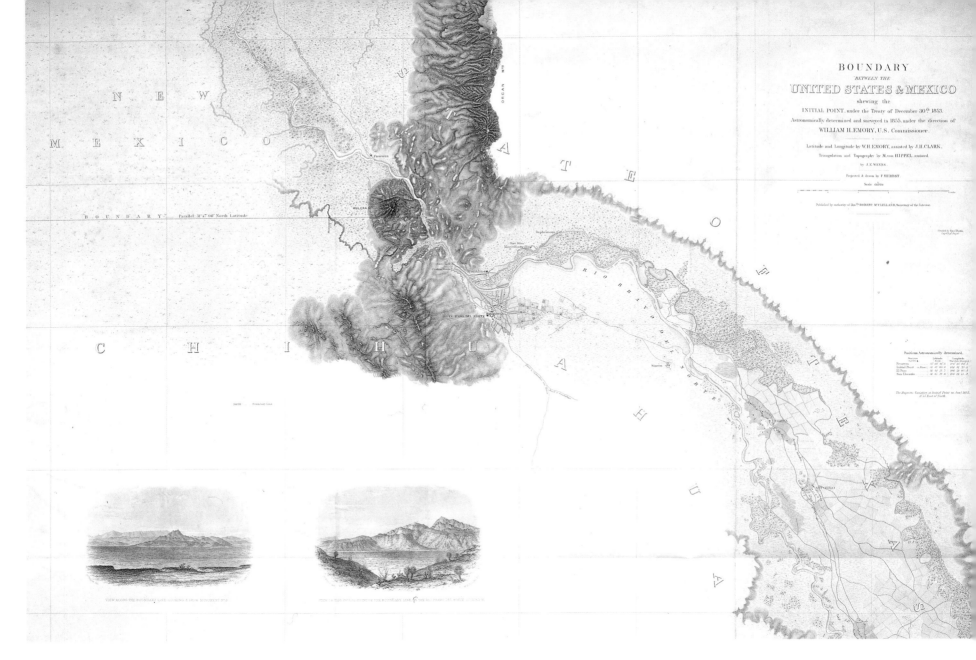

VIEW ALONG THE BOUNDARY LINE LOOKING E FROM MONUMENT N° 2.

VIEW OF THE INITIAL POINT ON THE BOUNDARY LINE 1/4 OF MI FROM DEL NORTE LOOKING W.

Newburyport, Massachusetts 1855

Left: Mention has already been made of the Anglo-American Fishery commission of 1862. This is a second chart from the series accompanying the report and shows the immediate approaches to the harbour of Newburyport, slightly to the north of Boston in Massachusetts, in 1855. It was another of the commercially produced charts adapted by the commission. Apart from the actual town, the chart also includes information about sea channels and had been annotated by the commissioners.

Mexico and New Mexico 1856

Left: This map illustrates the boundary between US and Mexico and shows the Initial Point under the treaty of 30 December 1853. It was surveyed in 1855 by William H. Emery, the United States Commissioner, assisted by J. H. Clark, M. von Hippel and J. E. Weyss. It was published by authority of the Honourable Robert McClelland, Secretary of the Interior. Although the bulk of New Mexico, California and Texas up to the Rio Grande had been ceded to the USA by Mexico as a result of the war of 1846-48, one final area was to be transferred at a later stage. This was the southernmost part of New Mexico — the so-called Gadsen Puchase of 1853 — which is the region illustrated here. The area measured some 30,000sq miles and cost $10 million

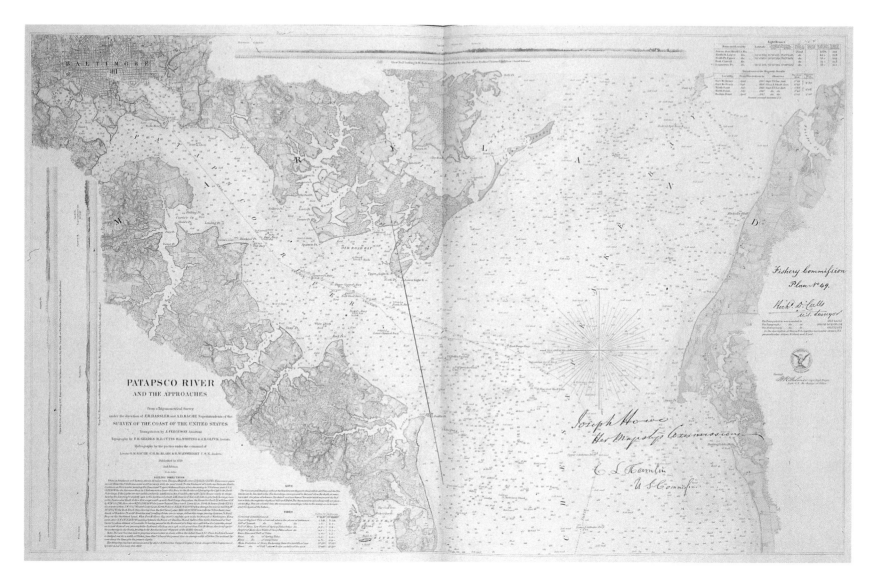

Patapsco River, Maryland 1859

Above: Drawn to a scale of three-quarters of a mile to one inch from a
trigonometrical survey undertaken under the direction of F. R. Hassler and
A. D. Bache (Superintendents of the Survey of the Coast of the United States)
in 1859, this map was one of a series incorporated in the Anglo-American
Fishery Commission's report of 1862. It shows the Patapsco River and the
approaches to Baltimore Harbor. Along with the maritime interest, the map
also shows roads, railways and field boundaries. The manuscript additions
delineate fishing limits and the map is endorsed by the commissioners.
Patapsco River is the broad stretch of water that links Baltimore with
Chesapeake Bay.

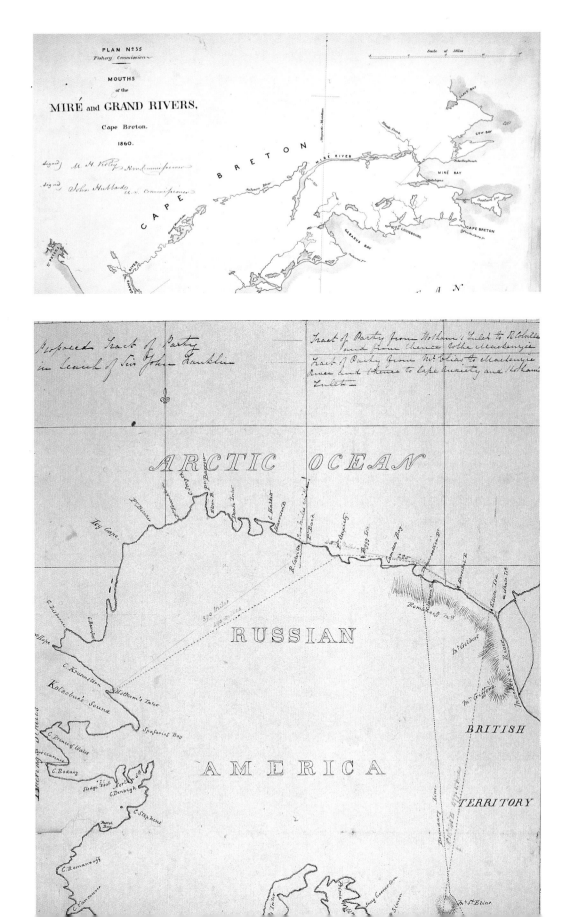

Miré and Grand Rivers 1860

Left: This is a third chart from the Anglo-American Fishery Commission of 1862 and is one of those charts drawn especially for the Commission. It shows the Miré and Grand Rivers on Cape Breton island in 1860. The island, situated just to the north of Nova Scotia — which, as Acadia, had been ceded by France to Britain after the Treaty of Utrecht in 1713 — on the approaches to the St Laurence remained French territory until the settlement of 1783, which saw the island transferred to British rule and its incorporation into Nova Scotia.

Alaska 1849

Left: The history of Alaska is subtly different to that of the rest of North America in that it was the Russians, rather than the British or French, who developed the region. It was in 1741 that Vitus Bering, a Dane after whom the Straits separating Alaska from Russia are named, discovered the south coast of the area later to be known as Alaska. Like a number of other explorers, Bering was not employed by his native country, but in his case by the Russians. In 1867, however, the Russians sold the territory to the USA for $7.2 million; the purchase, under the auspices of Secretary of State William H. Seward, was initially known as 'Seward's Folly' but, in the event, he was to be proved correct. The area's importance grew towards the end of the 19th century with the discovery of gold in the Yukon in 1897. Alaska became the 49th state of the Union in 1959 having achieved full territorial status in 1912. Thus, at the time that this map was compiled, the Russians held sway over the area. The map is annotated with the legend 'Proposed track of party in search of Sir John Franklin' and was filed with a report by Lt Sheard Osborn of the Royal Navy on 29 January 1849.

POTOMAC RIVER

AQUIA CREEK

BRENTS POINT

burg To Washington

ACCAKEEKI

RUN

Fredericksburg

BROOKS ST.

AQUIA LANDING

RICHMOND, FREDERICKSBURG, & POTOMAC R. R.

MARLBORO POINT

ACCAKEEK CREEK

POTOMAC CREEK

BELLE PLAIN

WAUG

FALMOUTH

PHILIPS HOUSE OVERLOOKING THE BATTLE FIELD GEN. BURNSIDES HEAD QUARTERS

GEN. FRANKLIN

Dr. TAYLOR'S HOUSE

MILL RACE

PAPER MILL

PONTOON BRIDGE CROSSED BY GEN. SUMNER

FALMOUTH STA.

LACY HOUSE FEDERAL BATTERIES COMMANDING THE TOWN

CLAIBORNE RUN

1862

FREDERICKSBURG

GEN. LONGSTREET AND LEE STANSBURY HILL

CONFEDERATE BATTERIES

PONTOON BRIDGE CROSSED BY GEN. HOOKER

PLANK ROAD

8 INCH RIFLE GUNS

HAZEL RUN

RAPPAHANNOCK RIVER

TELEGRAPH ROAD

To Richmond 60 Miles

RICHMOND, FREDERICKSBURG & POTOMAC R. R.

CONFEDERATE BATTERIES GEN. HILL

GEN. STONEWALL JACKSON

INTENDED FLANK MOVEMENT OF GEN. FRANKLIN

DEEP RUN

RIFLE PITS

LANE

SKINNERS NECK

BUCKNERS NECK

PONTOON BRIDGE CROSSED BY GEN. FRANKLIN

MASSAPONAX RIVER

BATTLE FIELD (*Dec. 13*) coloured th...

The Federal Right, under Gen. Sumner } "

The Federal Centre, under Gen. Hooker } "

The Federal Left, under Gen. Franklin } "

The Confederate Right, under Gens. 'Stonewall' Jackson and Hill }

The Confederate Left, under Gen. Longstreet } "

There were at this battle (in over *300.000* troops, either e... position,—*the Federals under G...* and the Confederates under Gen.

SCALE OF MILES

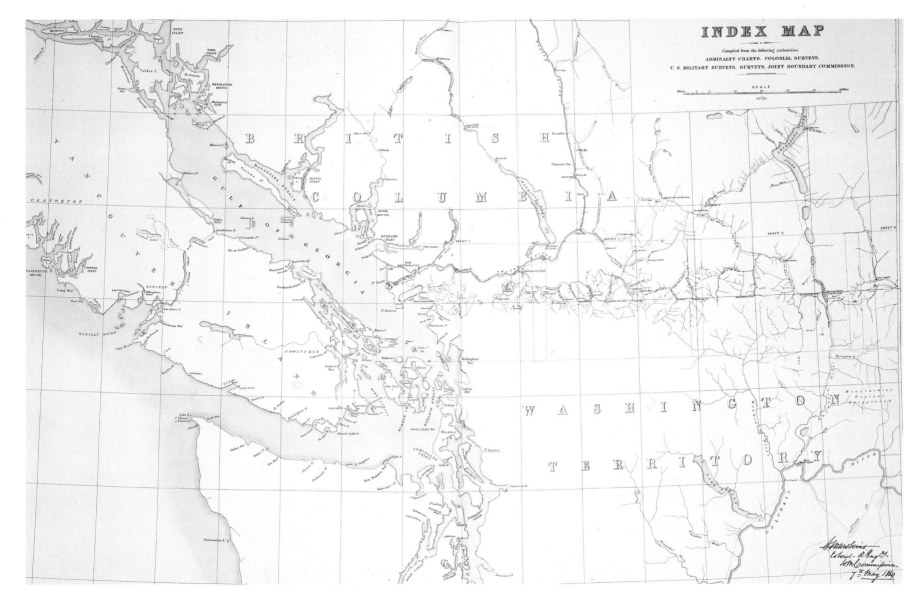

INDEX MAP

Compiled from the following authorities.
ADMIRALTY CHARTS. COLONIAL SURVEYS.
U. S. MILITARY SURVEYS. SURVEYS, JOINT BOUNDARY COMMISSION.

SCALE

Battle of Fredericksburg 1863

Left: Published by Bacon & Co, American Map Publishers, Paternoster Row, London, this map illustrates the disposition of forces during the Battle of Fredericksburg, Virginia. This battle, fought during the American Civil War, occurred on 13 December 1862. Shortly before the battle Abraham Lincoln had put Ambrose E. Burnside in control of the Union army; unfortunately, he was not one of the most successful of Union commanders and, in selecting to attack the Confederate forces entrenched in an uphill position, the Union army was defeated by the accuracy of the Confederate force's small arms fire, losing some 12,500 men and being forced to retreat northwards. The Confederate army was under the control of Robert E. Lee.

Canada 1869

Above: Although today we tend to see international boundaries as fixtures that have existed for hundreds of years, in truth the reality is very different, particularly in areas where European exploration and colonisation upset the previous land ownership patterns. This is true to a considerable extent in many of the artificial borders of the states and to the Canadian/United States border west of the Great Lakes. This area had been for many years a source of potential conflict between Britain and the USA and the final alignment, along the 49th parallel, was not agreed to until the Treaty of Washington on 15 June 1846. This is the index map covering the treaty boundary. The boundary had been surveyed and marked under the direction of a joint commission appointed to carry into effect the first article of the treaty. This version was reproduced by the Ordnance Survey in 1869 and has been endorsed by a colonel in the Royal Engineers, on behalf of Queen Victoria's commissioners. Although the boundary was fixed on the 49th parallel, the whole of Vancouver Island was allocated to Canada, with the boundary running between the lesser islands in the Gulf of Georgia.

Newfoundland 1881

Right: Published by Dangerfield of 22 Bedford Street, Covent Garden, London, this map has been annotated to mark the route of four Royal Navy ships — HMS *Druid*, HMS *Fantome*, HMS *Phoenix* and HMS *Contest* — on fishery patrol duties around the island. The annotated map, approved by Navigating Lieutenant W. J. N. Baird and Captain W. R. Kennedy, as senior officer, was enclosed with a letter sent to the British authorities on 31 October 1881. The original map is scaled at 18 miles to one inch. Each of the ship's routes is delineated in a separate colour and the detailed itinerary is in tabular form. Fishing was, until comparatively recently, one of the staple industries of the Newfoundland economy. A separate colony, Newfoundland was not to become part of Canada until after World War 2.

United States 1882

Far Right: Today, the existence of the nation's railway network is largely taken for granted and it is very easy to forget how important the growth of the railway industry was to the exploitation of the nation's natural resources and to the opening up of the Mid-West and to facilitating trans-continental travel. The original of the map illustrated here was sent as an enclosure with Consul Bridgett's Despatch Commercial No 6 from Galveston on 2 June 1883. Drawn to a scale of 70 miles to one inch and issued in 1892 by Rand, McNally & Co of Chicago (still one of the leading producers of maps in North America), the map portrays the Central Pacific Railroad and its leased lines and the lines of the Southern Pacific Railroad and its connections. The reference table describes completed lines, lines under construction or proposed, connecting lines and steamship lines. The Central Pacific Railroad was to be one of the companies involved in the construction of the first trans-continental railway. The Union Pacific Railroad had constructed westwards from the Mississippi basin while the Central Pacific Railroad had constructed eastwards from Sacramento. On 10 May 1869, the lines of the two companies were to meet at Promontory Point, Utah.

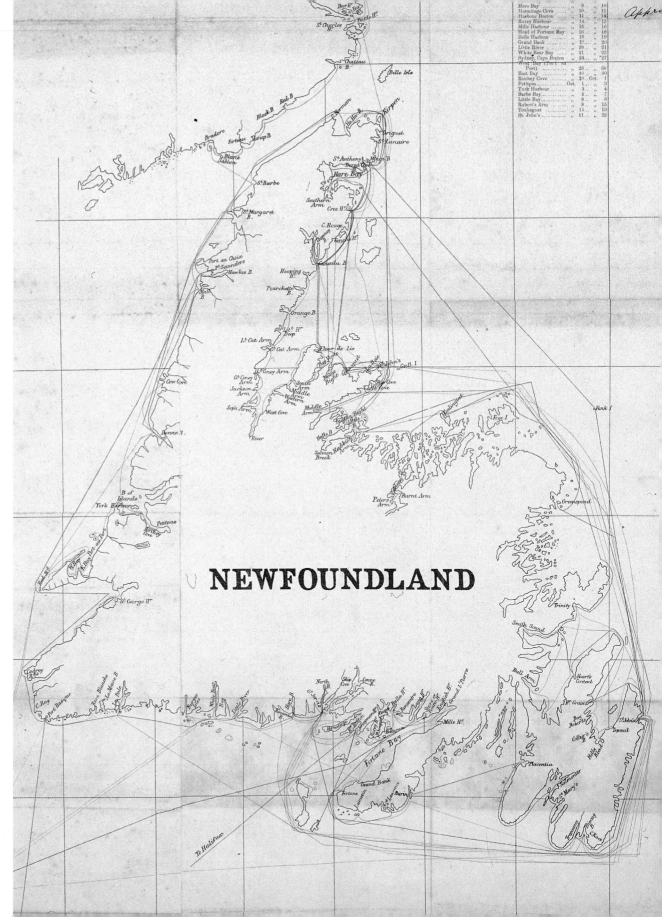

CENTRAL PACIFIC R'y
AND LEASED LINES
SOUTHERN PACIFIC R.R.
SEPTEMBER 1882   AND CONNECTIONS.

A. N. TOWNE,   T. H. GOODMAN,
General Manager.   Gen'l Pass. & Tkt. Agt.

REFERENCES.

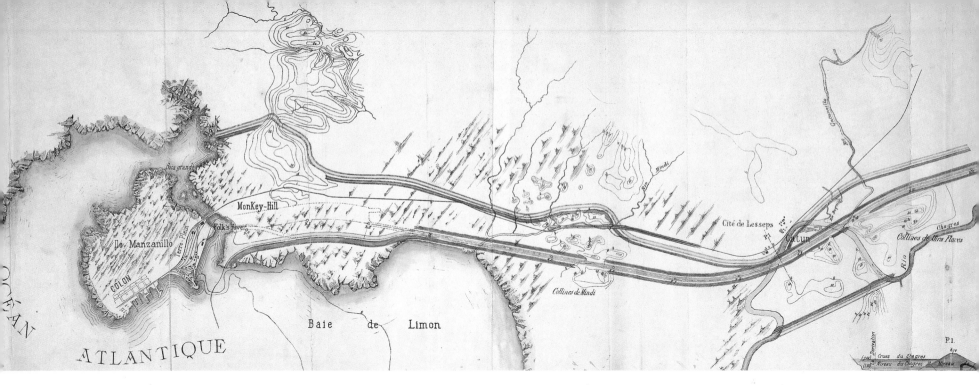

Fort Riley, Kansas 1891

Right: It was on 29 January 1861 that Kansas became the 34th state of the Union. This blueprint, one of a pair produced in 1891, shows the elevation for the construction of the military base at Fort Riley. These elevations show the quartermaster's and Commissioner's storehouse. They were drawn up by Capt J. W. Jacobs, Assistant Quartermaster of the US Army at Junction City, Kansas in 1892.

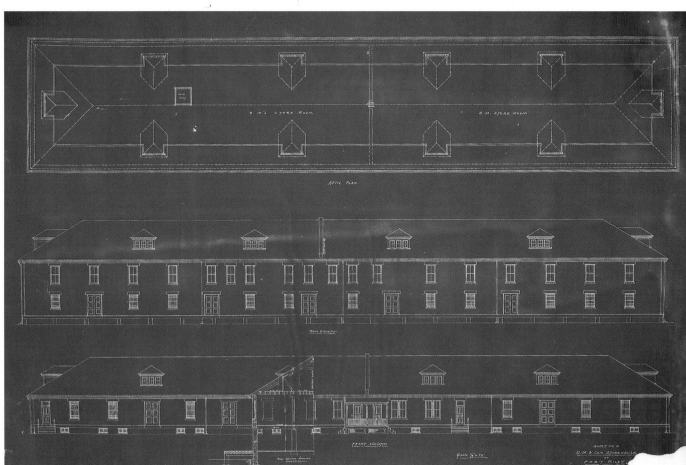

Panama 1886

Left: This is a section of a French map detailing preparatory work for the construction of a canal between the Pacific and Atlantic oceans. Described as '*Plan Topographique de la Region du canal dressé d'aprés les etudes faites par la Compaignie du Canal Interocéanic*' — a topographical plan drawn after the studies made for the company — the map shows in detail the preparatory work for the construction of the canal. In the event, it was not completed, but the idea of a canal through the Central American isthmus was not dead. In 1901, the USA and Britain agreed through the Hay-Pauncefote Treaty to the construction of a canal provided that it was open to the shipping of all nations. A second treaty, the Hay-Herrraán Convention of 1903, saw the United States agree with Columbia the payment of $10 million for a 99-year lease on a six-mile wide canal zone. In the event, this treaty was not ratified by Columbia. However, the Panamanians, aided by US support, revolted in November 1903 and threw out their Columbian overlords and signed the Hay-Bunau-Varilla Treaty with the United States later the same year. This gave the USA control of the canal zone and guaranteed Panamanian independence. With a seal in place, construction of the canal proceeded; it was opened on 15 August 1914.

Montreal 1907

Right: This highly detailed map of the harbour area in Montreal was first published by the Admiralty in 1860 and was subsequently revised in April 1892 and May 1899 before this version, which was issued in February 1907. The map shows in considerable detail the facilities available at the harbour, along with the connecting railways and streets. As a maritime chart, the map includes detailed information on the depth of the water and any potential hazards to shipping.

Index of maps